# FAMILY LIFE

# FAMILY LIFE

The most important values for living together

and raising children

## Jesper Juul

Translated by Hayes van der Meer

authorHOUSE®

*AuthorHouse™*
*1663 Liberty Drive*
*Bloomington, IN 47403*
*www.authorhouse.com*
*Phone: 1-800-839-8640*

*www.jesperjuul.com*
*www.family-lab.com*
*www.artofsayingno.tv*
*www.familylab.com.au*

*DVD Your Competent Child at www.textalk.se*
*Your Competent Child, published by Balboa Press*

*English titles published by AuthorHouse:*

*No!*
*Family Time*
*Here I am! Who are you?*

*Published by AuthorHouse    06/28/2012*

*ISBN: 978-1-4685-7927-7 (sc)*
*ISBN: 978-1-4685-7928-4 (hc)*
*ISBN: 978-1-4685-7929-1 (e)*

# Contents

# Introduction

Families everywhere are challenged by some degree of uncertainty. Thankfully, they are also motivated by curiosity and a genuine desire to find new ways. The traditional "until death do us part" family disappeared more than a generation ago. In most cultures, the nuclear family with its rigid separation of powers, roles and duties is also becoming something of the past. My own generation, the first after these breakdowns, persevered and held on to tradition with the help of a number of doctrines—and quite a few divorces.

It was actually not until around the turn of the century that relationships between couples, as well as the raising of children, had to be completely reinvented. It is important to remember that this reinvention is being done by every single couple as they are not able or willing to copy their parents' ways of doing things. Neither do they have any significant role models.

The modern family is no longer always defined as a father, a mother and one or more children. Single parenting is not necessarily an expression of social unhappiness or romantic failure. The patchwork family with mine, yours and/or our children has flourished, and the divorced father or mother who is with his or her children on a shared basis also makes up a family in a psychological and existential sense. In addition to this, there are homosexual couples with or without children, adoptive families, foster families and shared households with multiple generations under one roof.

What we are talking about here is a far more significant transformation than the traditional generational changes of the past. This has obviously resulted in a greater degree of uncertainty. Add to this the fact that more children spend more time than ever in institutional care outside of the family. In Scandinavia more than 90% of parents have themselves spent approximately 25,000 childhood hours in educational institutions or other daycare arrangements. Many have, for better or worse, had a greater exposure to professional pedagogy than they have to traditional family upbringing. This is why recent years have been marked by parents questioning every important—and not so important—issue.

"What should we do if our two year old won't go to sleep when she's been put to bed?"

"What do you do when a 10 year old wants a body piercing?"

"Our four year old refuses to eat vegetables. What should we do?"

"There is total chaos every morning. Are we bad parents, is it just us or do others experience the same things?"

"I prefer to avoid conflicts. Is that wrong?"

"When my husband is alone with the kids he never has the same problems as I do. Is he missing something—or am I?"

"My partner wants peace and quiet when we eat, but isn't that too harsh on the kids?"

"We almost never talk anymore. What should we do?"

"A good sex life is important to me, but at this stage my husband only wants to have sex once a month. Do I just have to accept that?"

This uncertainty and search for understanding is neither new nor is it something unique to today's families. Parents have always been insecure. The difference is perhaps that today's parents generally are admirably open about their uncertainty. We no longer live in a world where everyone knows what "one" does and thereby what is "right" and "wrong." Just a generation ago we lived in relatively isolated communities characterized largely by a values-related consensus that essentially was morally based. What does one do and what not? What is a duty and what should we do?

In 1960, when I was 12 years old, I asked my parents for permission to go to a jazz club. There was no hesitation and no uncertainty in the resounding "No, certainly not!" When I dared to ask for a reason, their answer was: "People don't do that at your age, end of discussion." Later I would verify this claim with my peers and I found out that my parents were in fact right. No 12 year olds were allowed into the club. For my parents and their contemporaries, this knowledge of what one does was a great support, which was further strengthened by one of their own principal values: one does not deviate from what one does.

Today's parents have to deal with highly complex and challenging situations. They have to answer the 12 year old who wants to get her belly button pierced, who wants his cell phone subscription financed or who has come home drunk from a party. These are not easy situations to deal with and relating to what one does or does not do only lasts as long as it takes the child to exchange a few SMS messages or e-mails with his or her friends. Their in-box will soon be able to verify that there are actually some people who do and who are allowed to do so. Parents have to be preemptive and ask around. They have to talk to parents in similar situations, ask experts, consult the school nurse or the school counselor. Even then they might still feel uncertain simply because the "experts" do not always agree.

Before the 1960s the leaders of society had some relatively clear ideas about which values were most important in the public debate, in school education and pedagogy. Political ideologies as well as religious teachings played an important role as the shared moral foundation. Today, with few exceptions, it is difficult to tell the difference between the political parties, their basic values and their view of human nature—that is, if they actually have one. Even the most extreme parties often define themselves more by what they are against than what they have in common with others. From a family point of view none of them have anything to say that is progressive. There is not much which supports life within the family or connects family life with the world outside. In general, schools suffer from the same uncertainty and conflict/problem-oriented focus. To a great extent, the Church in many countries finds it difficult to formulate its otherwise very good values in ways which resonate with people and make good common sense. If we analyze which values dominate the structures of our society, the answer will be: the market's values. Therefore, an important question is whether or not it is at all possible to understand oneself as a person without also understanding the market, its structures, philosophies and mechanisms.

The values which dominate the market (and its lack of respect for human nature) cannot be used as a foundation for a family's life together. Yet, the market's ideas have slowly but surely infiltrated our understanding of our own private lives. The possibilities for two people to join as a couple is largely determined by their abilities to market themselves at bars, clubs, on the Internet and other places where singles meet to check out and try out the selection. There is an alarming and growing number of suicides among white, Western European women who do not think they can live with the fact that their breast size, genitals or the length of their legs can live up to the marketplace's perception of what is ideal. To a disturbing degree children are being reduced to objects and commodities. Not only are children sold—destined for sexual abuse, illegal adoption and delivery of healthy organs to ill, wealthy adults to an extent not seen before—but we ordinary, law-abiding citizens have virtually agreed that it ought to be a society-financed human right to have children even if we are unable to have them ourselves. If one then becomes pregnant with twins, the right to get rid of one fetus is being discussed in complete earnestness, and now the time is drawing nearer where an order can be placed with specific requirements regarding height, gender, eye color, intelligence and so forth. A couple has in fact insisted they had the right to return an adopted child because they fell pregnant several years after the adoption. Adoption agencies experience that adoptive parents-to-be choose not to take children who do not live up to the family's own self-image. For years institutions have labeled children and young people as either well-functioning or poorly functioning as though they were describing a kitchen appliance that met or did not live up to certain standardization criteria. So far it has been an ethical slide without many curves or obstacles and there is no indication that this is going change. In other words, this is what our values have become. As long as medical technology or criminal organizations will provide the supply, demand is not a problem. The market is like that, it is how it all operates. The question is whether or not we will accept our families to operate by those same standards?

In exactly the same way as children have become one of our many possible choices, so have relationships, marriages and living together. These are no longer social or moral necessities but personal choices. There is every reason to celebrate this. No one is—or should be—forced to live with another person with whom they are not happy or by whom they are oppressed and abused. Values have changed from "one has to stick together at all costs, especially if one has children" to "one has to take oneself seriously". Later in this book we will look at how these two statements are not necessarily in conflict with each other.

It is part of the market-oriented culture to talk about tools, models, concepts and methods and these things are what questioning parents quite superficially are asking for when they are searching for answers. The problem however is that a method which fits everyone cannot be found. We human beings and our relationships are far too dissimilar for that to be possible. I know this must sound surprising coming from someone who has lived his entire professional life in the experts' marketplace, which is teeming with methods, concepts and ready-made solutions. Nonetheless, this is what I have always believed. There is no objective psychological or pedagogical support for using generalized tricks and tips.

People are not machines so the use of tools and techniques is precluded. There is—from a values-related point of view—a huge difference between asking "What techniques exist to get children to sleep?" and asking "What qualities and skills do I need to develop so my child can sleep peacefully?" Or "Aren't there any techniques that can get women to give up their resistance to sex?" and "Our sex life has slowed down—too much in my opinion. How can I talk to my wife so that she doesn't just feel criticized and loses her desire even more?" The same can be said about methods. They work—of course they do—but only as long as one party accepts being reduced to an object.

People develop poorly and do not thrive when they are subjected to concepts. For example, children who have grown up in an Israeli kibbutz or a kindergarten in the Soviet Union, just to take two completely different ideological points of reference.

Most of us have an idea of what our future family is supposed to look like but we are only going to succeed if we allow the idea to evolve and we recognize that the family is made up of living people. Concepts are a kind of mini religion—they work only as long as the congregation is willing to submit to the inventor (pastor) and they have a low tolerance for dissidents.

The fundamental problem with methods is that, in principle, they work according to plan, especially if the adults stand together and the family lives a relatively isolated life. Methods work, not because they are good, but simply because children have an incredible ability to cooperate and a willingness to accommodate the adults they love and depend on. Children's ability to cooperate is considerable. Even as adults they copy their own parents' methods of upbringing, in spite of the fact that they themselves might have suffered great pain. That is why issues such as physical abuse, psychological violence and sexual abuse are part of what we call the negative social legacy.

Physical violence is without doubt one of the most effective methods of raising children—if effective means that the adults get what they want as quickly as possible. Simply visit families or countries where it is still acceptable to use violence against children and see how quickly they can be made to eat food they do not like or eat more than they have the appetite for. See how quickly they will stop protesting when they are treated unfairly. And see how quickly a child is able to close their eyes and lie completely still when threatened even though they just a few seconds before refused to go to bed. It is indeed easy for us as parents to get things our way but we also get young people and adults who are stunted in their bodies and souls. These are destructive relationships between parents and children, but if those are our shared values then everybody can live with them. That is part of the power, which also is part of strong common values.

We cannot live satisfying lives if we live according to the path of least resistance or if we must ask others for advice and guidance every single time we face new conflicts or problems. It is both humiliating and extremely tiring to walk around constantly feeling uncertain. It leaves a very real mark on the relationship between parents and children. Nevertheless, it is what more and more parents attempt to do. Their interactions with children and young people move from one conflict to the next. They understandably hope and search for solutions that are specifically tailored to the issues relating to sleep, food, bed times, going to school, alcohol abuse and so on. However those tailored solutions do not exist. There are some overriding principles and values that can guide us in the direction of individual solutions. Some of those are what we will look at in this book.

The alternative to living in fear of the conflicts that might be waiting or struggling to avoid them means that we must have some kind of sorting mechanism—something which can distinguish between good and bad. It must be able to sort the input we receive from the outside such as experts, parents, friends and family—and the things we are able to define ourselves by. For this we need a measuring stick which must be made up of our values. To a great extent we have to invent and reinvent the relationships with our partners and evaluate and adjust the way we raise our children. Add to this the fact that we ourselves have to consider millions of questions which used to be answered by society's values-related consensus. This consensus is no longer available and nobody is able to cope with all those decisions on their own. This is why a values-based measuring stick is important.

Let me illustrate this with a current problem: more and more children and young people are becoming overweight to a degree that not only threatens their own health and well-being, it also burdens the economy.

The major cause of this problem stems from over-consumption of very sugary soft drinks, fattening snacks, junk food and fast food. Before the 1980s children had very little access to these things or they simply did not exist. Now they are a natural part of their daily consumption. Something similar is occurring in the adult world. Party food and drinks used to be consumed only rarely—perhaps on a monthly basis. These days however they are often daily treats.

Parents today face a real challenge to regulate their children's consumption of products that are dangerous to their health. Even if they had every authority and every political party behind them, it would not provide them with much support in the inevitable conflicts with those children and young people who have either already built up a significant consumption or who watch with envy as their friends are given permission. In these situations it does not make any substantial impression on their children when their parents refer to a governmental health department as the authority. Parents must find the authority within themselves, and that is what is called values.

What is meant by values? The answer is twofold: they are the thoughts and ideas that really matter to us. The second part is that they add value to our lives and leave their mark on our daily actions and reflections. In a family—a love-based community—the most important question is:

"How can I convert my loving feelings into positive actions, which those near to me will also experience as loving—without losing my personal integrity?"

Our values and principles cannot answer this existential question in detail but they can serve as points of reference and guide us in our continuous attempts to discover and re-discover the answer. Values are not the same as goals. They exist both before and after the goal has been met. The values describe our journey towards that goal and the qualities of that journey rather than the goal itself.

The values described in the following are not mine, neither have I made them up. They stem from many sources, and my contribution is limited to the gathering and giving some of them new names and meanings. You might think they are a bit anemic but I wanted to limit myself to the values which create mental and social health. This applies to people who are growing up and to adults who continue developing through interaction with other people. Those are the values I know best. You can further build on this foundation with the philosophical, religious, political, cultural and spiritual values you might find useful.

I have had the privilege of meeting families from many different countries and cultures and can confidently state that the following four fundamental values transgress across any culture. They can function as guides for any parent with small children, as well as for second generation children of immigrants and refugees who are split between their own ideas and their parents values. These values can, in the same way, successfully function as a link between partners in the quickly growing group of so-called mixed marriages between people of different national and ethnic origins. The only thing it requires is that the parties do not resort to hopeless arguments about what is the "right" thing to do when the child will not sit still at the table, refuses to do his homework or comes home too late. The challenge is rather to reflect on the central values. Every experience tells us that it is much better for our peace of mind when values determine our actions as supposed to when they are merely after-rationalizations in disguise.

The values described in this book do not differentiate between men or women, adults or children, young or old. This is not to ignore the countless and important differences there are, but in order to emphasize our shared human nature—the highest common denominators.

The book is built up in such a way that the first four chapters describe the values concepts which are related to a number of practical examples from everyday family life. The principles that naturally follow from these values concepts are described and discussed. The values are not prioritized by importance since, in my opinion, they are equally important, but they are in the order that seems most logical in relation to the content and the way in which they depend upon each other. The last two chapters describe where the values must function: in community and through parental leadership..

It is always exciting, stimulating and at times even provoking to discuss one's own values and those of others. Not least because we, through these discussions, often discover that our values are in fact different to the way we thought or wished they were. Which values do you and I have from the families we grew up in? Which values were formulated and which were implicit? How many of these values were actually practiced in our families and which were mostly "decoration"? Many companies and institutions also have such debates about their values. Subsequently they have had to acknowledge that values are much easier to formulate than to transform into action.

That is also what most families will experience. It may take years before the actual practice begins to resemble the ideals of what you want to happen. We do not begin to respect each other simply because we think it is right to respect others. We often overlook the other person's need for support even though we firmly believe that mutual support is one of the family's most important functions. If that was not the case we could make do with the golden rules of the Bible: "Love thy neighbor as thyself!" and "Treat others the way you want them to treat you!"

For generations the underlying problem has been that most people deep down have an unloving relationship with themselves and treat themselves poorly. In my experience this is neither due to laziness nor individual immaturity but it is rather due to a kind of collective immaturity. As human beings we have not been able to develop psychologically and socially at the same rate as the world has developed.

Perhaps part of the explanation can be found in the discoveries made by brain researchers who have found that the human brain has not developed over the past 50,000 years! In any case, most of us are aware that our social and cultural veneer often is terribly thin and the distance between empathy and raw primitiveness frighteningly short. This is not only so for those who have had a so-called unhappy childhood marked by inhumane and destructive values. This is also true for you and I and those with whom we live. Therefore, we might be able to explore and formulate our values as part of the process of our personal development. Even the families we are members of are, in reality, simple expressions of our collective values-related ideas for the future.

It would not be in the spirit of this book or my personal beliefs if you interpret my suggestions as absolute truths or some kind of religious belief system. They are not. If everybody in your family is thriving and doing well, there is really no reason for making any adjustments. However, if you are left with some degree of uncertainty and a sense of powerlessness, my experiences can hopefully be useful and inspire you. Living together and raising children is in many ways a lifelong experiment that nobody gets through without making daily mistakes. Life is certainly not about getting things right—let alone being perfect. It is all about trying to make some kind of sense out of all the madness. One way of doing this is to translate your personal values into your daily life. Perhaps you are able to do this with someone who is important to you and to whom you are important.

# Equal dignity

When we enter into a relationship and start a family we carry the genes and personalities which have shaped us thus far. We are the way we are—as they say. To express this more succinctly—we grow out of our childhood and adolescent years with two types of behaviors—an inner behavior, which refers to our thoughts and emotions, and an outer behavior, which refers to the way in which we act in relation to other people. The difference between our inner and outer behavior is often significant. At times however, there is concurrence between what we think, how we feel and what we show the outside world through our verbal and physical expressions. The two types of behaviors are constructive (for ourselves and our interactions with others) and self-destructive (for ourselves and always for the people who care about us.)

Most of us are immature when we enter a relationship and start a family. This is not meant as a criticism and does not refer to child-like behavior. It is rather an acknowledgement of the fact that we really do not know ourselves all that well and are lacking insight into our two types of behavior—the constructive and the self-destructive. The maturation process does not pick up speed and take shape until we enter into new and binding relationships.

Regardless of what kind of family we are referring to, the key word is therefore relations—or relationships. It is the quality of these relations/relationships that determine how well we thrive and how well we are able to develop as human beings. When adult partners fail to thrive it is not because there is something wrong with them or with their partner—neither do children fail to thrive because they have bad parents. We fail to thrive when what goes on between us does not contain the right elements or qualities, as I prefer to call them, regardless of whether they are constructive or destructive. One of the most important qualities is equal dignity.

Equal dignity does not mean that we are being equally matched nor is it the same as equality. In my understanding, equal dignity means that "both are of the same value" (as people) and "with the same respect for each other's personal dignity and integrity".

Equal dignity in a relationship therefore means that the wishes of both, their opinions and needs, are treated with the same gravity by the community and are not rejected or put down with reference to gender, age or disability. What you say is valuable to the community simply because you are you, because you are a human being and because you are an important part of this relation. With this approach, equal dignity refers to all people's fundamental need to be seen, heard and taken seriously as individuals.

Hence, equal dignity is the only real alternative to traditional patriarchal family patterns where the official ranking order was clear—the man and father at the top, then the woman and mother and thereafter the children. This type of family clearly reflected the division of power in society, but just as in society, it was not only about power, it was also about allocation of responsibilities. The man was the provider. With "his" money came the power. One follows the other. Physical and mental care for the children, the home and the rest of the family was built into the woman's role. When this family functioned best, it functioned as a harmonious and enlightened despotism. As women became educated, employed and earned money they obviously demanded part of the power and a more equal division of the responsibilities. However, it quickly became evident that it was not quite that simple.

When that important reorganization of the family took place, citizens in western democracies also rebelled against authorities, demanded genuine democracy and requested greater transparency in the public arena. It is therefore no wonder that people for some time regarded democratic values as a usable alternative to the family's enlightened despotism—but they are not! Democratic values are essential as the sounding board of human relations but they do not suffice within the family because they only deal with the distribution of power. They do not take into account the feelings and the care which is the essential quality of the family. In society, the majority holds the power. The caretaker role (= the social and health sector) has markedly lower status than the provider role (= business life). The family must care equally well for the minority as for others. Conversely, a family cannot thrive if the power is delegated to the majority—especially not if the children make up this majority. In a family, the adults are, and should be, in charge. They hold the economic and the social power. Just as importantly, the adults hold the psychological power, the responsibility for the tone, atmosphere and mood and they hold the power to maintain or change this. In families where this responsibility is handed over to the children all parties develop poorly and will fail to thrive. Many modern parents do not feel comfortable being in charge of the children and young people. They would rather avoid using their power. That is unfortunate, because although children are born with great wisdom, they are born without experience. Therefore they need the experience and leadership of the adults. In this respect families resemble other organizations. It is devastating for the group's well-being and productivity when those who are in charge pretend not to be.

The real question is not whether the adults have the power, but how they choose to use it, and that is where equal dignity comes in as the most constructive value.

To feel treated with equal dignity is the opposite of being talked down to, lectured to, voted down, labeled or made fun of. It has nothing to do with niceness or reason. We can certainly treat each other with equal dignity—even when we are furious or sad. Nothing prevents us from doing that—except perhaps if we are not able to treat ourselves with dignity.

Equal dignity primarily expresses itself through language. A dialog which is based on equal dignity is a conversation in which both parties express themselves, their own thoughts, values, feelings, dreams and goals instead of theorizing or talking about each other.

After reading the above, many readers might think "Yes, that's all well and good in theory, but it's impossible in practice. People aren't like that!" This is true, in some ways. We are thoroughly irrational beings who are also full of envy, jealously, self-centeredness, inferiority, arrogance and megalomania. The problem is that all of these feelings individually and together can ruin any meaningful relationship with other people. Therefore, we are on a collision course with ourselves and some aspects of our human nature, namely our inescapable need to be part of a meaningful community.

Janus (aged 3): I'm hungry!

Mother: That's ridiculous. We had lunch just an hour ago—you can't be hungry already!

This is a typical expression of parental care at its most degrading, steamrolling and dictatorial. Here are a number of different possible answers based on equal dignity:

"That's amazing! We almost just finished eating. Are you really hungry?"

"Have you asked your tummy . . . does it really say that? Try to ask it again."

"That was fast! I'm not going to give you anything for another two hours. Your appetite has gotten so big that it's not good for you, and we need to make it smaller. Let's see whether we can figure out something else for you to think about so your tummy doesn't shout quite so loud."

"What an appetite you have today! What would you like to eat?

Gosh, that's too bad, because I don't have time right now to get you something. You'll have to wait until I'm done folding our washing."

A Danish woman living in France and married to a Frenchman is troubled by the use of physical violence in French families and their institutions for children. She tries to talk to her husband about it but he is inclined to defend his country, his parents and their culture. The dispute develops and eventually she sees no other option than to move back to Denmark with the children.

The situation is unfortunate because both parents are left thinking that the other has assumed power and is abusing it. In a culturally mixed marriage like this the concept of equal dignity means that the family can be neither French nor Danish. Both parents are prevented from copying the families they grew up with and ultimately they must create a completely new kind of family with cross-cultural values. Often they will find themselves in situations where some of their childhood values have to give way for more general values—in this case the two most important values: equal dignity and care for personal integrity. Violence against children or adults certainly can be ingrained in a culture but that does not make it less destructive or degrading for the person who is affected. Therefore, traditional cultural values must give way.

This type of conflict does not necessarily have to be about violence against children—and it occurs in any cultural mix. A mother or a father might be unhappy about the conditions at their child's daycare centre. The other parent might not agree but it is the satisfied parent's obligation to be prepared to support finding a solution that both of them can live with. Not out of an insincere sense of caring for the child, but out of caring for the partner and the equal dignity between them. (This was in fact the real reason why the two adults in this example divorced—not the violence, which is part of French child-raising.) When two people live together in a love-based relationship their relationship is, in fact, their first shared "child". If their fundamental values do not mark their mutual relationship then the effort of trying to pass them on to biological offspring is a futile exercise.

She: I'm fed up with the fact that I have to do 80% of the work around here. That wasn't what we agreed on and I think it's really lousy that you just expect that I'll take care of everything.

He: Wait a minute, 80% is not exactly right. I do as damn much as I possibly can, but I also need to work and relax every once in awhile.

She: And I don't . . . ? I also have a job and I have the kids most of the time, don't I! When am I supposed to relax? Can you tell me that?

He: Yeah OK, I can see that, but I don't know what we should do about it . . . maybe we could get somebody to clean house a couple times a week like Robert and Helen. That's been a good solution for them, hasn't it?

She: You don't know what we should do about it?! You just need to get off your butt and do your share of the work. That's what we need to do about it! Or maybe you also want to hire a cook and a babysitter and a gardener. Tell me . . . is it a family you want or an institution? I think you should sit back and think a bit about that while you relax!

He: Why do you always need to exaggerate? I'm just trying to be constructive . . . you're the one who's so goddamned dissatisfied.

This argument is completely without equal dignity, not only in the way the two speak together but also in regards to what they talk about. She complains and criticizes her partner instead of saying what she wants. This is inappropriate. He defends himself instead of answering, which is inappropriate too.

This issue is about who looks after the practical tasks within the family. After the partial dissolution of the traditional gender roles most people have agreed that the adults in principle should share the tasks approximately 50:50—especially if both have jobs outside of the home. Nevertheless, in reality men and women still lug around the gender roles of the past where his role was to provide for the family. In return the family was supposed to offer him the requisite service, rest and recreation. Her role was to be responsible for the food, children, house-keeping and, in addition, everything that creates the mood and atmosphere in the home.

Responsibility is a very complicated issue, which cannot easily be scheduled. As long as we are burdened by history like the couple in the previous example, it is necessary that the man enters a relationship with the clear assumption that he himself is responsible for putting food in his mouth, clothes on his body and maintaining a reasonable hygienic standard—at a minimum. The woman must be careful to curb her caring gene and ensure she does not assume an over-responsible role otherwise she will end up doing more than is good for her. Families have started this transition but it will presumably take a long time. As a starting point, both of them must agree that each of them need to take care of themselves. One partner might do the shopping and cooking every day or take on the responsibility for doing the laundry and ironing. This is to be considered a gift to the relationship, and not a given or part of an implied tradeoff. With this starting point we can envision two alternative versions of the previous argument.

Version 1:

She: I need to speak with you about something. I feel I have taken on too much of the practical work in our family—more than I can cope with. It makes me grumpy and unhappy and I don't want to do it anymore. So I want to talk to you about how we can arrange things differently.
He: Wait a minute, I do as much as I possibly can . . .
She: I'm not saying that you don't do enough, but that I do too much. That's why I want us to find another solution together.
He: And what's that supposed to be?
She: I don't know. Actually, I'd prefer that we each think about it on our own for a couple days. Then we can sit down and look at each of our possible solutions. Otherwise

I'm afraid that solving the problem will also become my responsibility.

In this version the woman attends to her responsibility and looks after her own dignity. Thereby she avoids being accusatory, degrading and critical whereas the man is still on the defensive, he is passive and without consideration for her well-being and the quality of their mutual relationship. His lack of effort with regard to the family's practical tasks is reflected in his passive way of participating in the conversation. This might be the way he is or maybe he just does not like talking about cleaning and dishwashing. Regardless, she has now offered him the opportunity to reestablish his dignity by giving him time to formulate some solutions. The division of the roles between them jeopardizes their relationship which is why it is sensible for them to prioritize equal dignity higher than the dishwashing—for a while at least.

Version 2:

She: I need to speak with you about something. I feel I have taken on too much of the practical work in our family—more than I can cope with. It makes me grumpy and unhappy, and I don't want to do it anymore. So I want to talk to you about how we can arrange things differently.

He: I wasn't aware of that . . . To be completely honest, I hadn't even noticed. What can I do?

She: Right now you can just talk to me about it, and then of course we need to figure out some way of making things work. I can understand that you haven't noticed because it's something I've just been doing quietly for a long time, so I didn't discover it until I began to get mad at you about all kinds of little things.

He: Yeah, that I have noticed!

She: I'm not trying to turn our family into a democracy with every little thing, but I take on too much responsibility too quickly and end up feeling totally alone. It's crappy for me, and it ruins our relationship. You're simply going to have to help me be less overly responsible and take on more responsibility yourself. That's the only solution I can see.

He: Yeah, but it's hard—also because you're so fast. And I bust my butt at work . . .

She: Yes, I realize that, but the fact that there's lots to do at work doesn't mean there's less responsibility at home. In any case, I'm not willing to go on like this, and I want you to come with a suggestion for a new division of responsibilities. I don't want to be the employer here at home.

He: So you're not just frustrated. This is serious?

She: Yes!

In this version equal dignity is in place. She has taken responsibility for her own situation and drawn attention to the needs of the relationship. He has laid his cards on the table. Time will tell how he can mobilize his responsibility and consideration. They have, in other words, had a personal dialog on equal terms instead of a fight or an argument. In a dialog the parties speak from their own points of reference. This personal dialog has two qualities. It takes good care of their relationship and it clarifies it. At the same time it leaves room for maximum creativity in preparation for finding new perspectives and solutions. The fight destroys the relationship and prevents joint solutions. When people start talking about each other instead of speaking for themselves, fights arise. We must remember that arguments end with a winner and a loser which may initially be good for the winner—but it is a fragile and short-lived ceasefire. Arguments are always about the topic and ignore, therefore, the most important thing—the personal aspect.

Pia (age 12): I'd really like to get my eyebrow pierced. Just like Malene . . . only a little piercing.

Mother: I might as well tell you straight away that you're not going to get my permission! You're far too young to be able to foresee the consequences, and it looks terrible, anyway. I simply cannot understand why Malene was allowed.

Pia: But can't we just talk about it? We can also wait until dad gets home?

Mother: There's nothing to talk about Pia—I thought I'd already said that. And by the way, dad has to go to a meeting tonight so don't even try to go down that road. You shouldn't always just try to be like everybody else.

Pia: Why can't we just talk about it? What about your tattoo? You were allowed to get that when you were young.

Mother: I was 17 years old and didn't need to get permission and I've regretted getting that tattoo many times since. You are way too immature for that kind of thing. End of story!

Pia: Jesus Christ, you're so old-fashioned!

Mother: Don't you talk to me like that, young lady. Don't be a smart aleck! Go to your room and do your homework until it's time for dinner!

Pia: I'd frigging well rather go there—at least it's my room!

Not a very a very productive outcome. The mother "won" but both of them lost, really. At some later stage Pia might be able to talk her parents into getting a piercing, maybe she will have one done without their approval or maybe she will not get one at all. This is not important. What matters is that the relationship between the two has been weakened because Pia has been steamrolled by her mother's attitude to piercing. It will without doubt make her reluctant to share a number of her other wishes, dreams, thoughts and experiences. Besides, the mother makes frequent use of what we call her adult defining power—that is, the power to label children, pigeonhole them and decide what and who they are. (Pia is "too young", "immature" and a "smart aleck"). This is probably the most frequently used, but also the most destructive way of violating a child's integrity. The defining power is also often used when two adults argue—and then it is just as destructive to the quality of the relationship.

Pia's mother clearly lacked insight into this, very quickly delivered a moral condemnation and added a punishment when the daughter gave her a taste of her own medicine by defining her as "old-fashioned".

An alternative conversation based on equal dignity:

Pia (age 12): I'd really like to get my eyebrow pierced. Just like Malene . . . only a little piercing.

Mother: Oh no! That's one thing I hoped you'd never ask me.

Pia: Yeah, but . . . Malene's parents let her, so if you just say "Yes!" you're awesome! It's not very expensive, and I have enough money.

Mother: Sit down for a minute and take a deep breath. Just the fact that Malene has one isn't quite good enough for me. I'd like to hear why you want to?

Pia: Yeah, but . . . it's cool. Can't you understand that?

Mother: Yes, I suppose I can if I really make an effort, but . . . "cool" isn't quite enough . . .

Pia: But I want to so much . . . everybody is getting it done.

Mother: I can understand this thing about everybody is getting it done, and you want to be like everybody else, but you usually have your own individual thoughts about that kind of stuff. That's what I want to hear about.

Pia: Oh! Malene just got hers done yesterday, and it's not the kind of thing you go and think about. It's just something you feel like doing. Can't you understand that?

Mother: Yes, I understand that, but I don't feel like giving you permission, and that's why you'd better come up with something better. Think about it, and in the meantime I'll talk with your father, and we'll see.

Pia: Yeah, but when . . ?

Mother: I can't give you an answer to that. But it won't be tomorrow or the next day.

Pia: Aaargh. It's so annoying the way grown-ups always have to think and think . . .

Mother: Yes, I'm sure it is, but that's just the way we are.

It is not about whether Pia is given permission or not. It is about having a dialog where both of them feel heard and taken seriously. That is why Pia has to qualify her reasoning and that is why her mother has to take a closer look at her immediate aversion to piercing. After that, they need to talk again and maybe again and again. If the final answer is "No!" Pia will be disappointed and perhaps angry with her parents, but no harm comes of that. It is simply lesson no. 2000 about the fact that within a family everyone must be free to say what they want, without it being certain that they get what they want. In principle, there is no difference between who wants what—whether it is the two-year-old who wants an ice cream, the father who wants peace and quiet, the mother who wants to be courted or the 19 year old who wants his parents to co-sign a car loan. It is never the topic itself or its relative importance that determines the quality of the decision making process. It is the importance it has for the one who is asking.

Kim (age 2): Daddy, can I have an ice cream?

Father: No, not now.

Kim: But I really want one!

Father: Yes, I can hear that you want one, Kim, and it's OK that you want to have an ice cream, but I won't give you one!

Kim: Stupid Dad!

Father: Yes, I understand you think that, but that's how it's going to be.

The equal dignity in this dialog lies not only in what has been said but just as much in what is not being said. These are some of the messages, which were not communicated:

"You've had enough ice cream for today!"
(Adult defining power.)

"I've said no, so stop pestering me about it!"
(I don't dare to say no openly, so I better make you feel wrong because you openly argue for what you want.)

"But if you're really good, maybe we can have ice cream for dessert tonight."
(Doesn't dare say a clear no, but uses a cheap diversionary tactic instead.)

"You want this and you want that. Do you think everybody else gets stuff just because they want it? That's not how it works here, young man!"
(In this family you'd better be careful asking for what you want. You risk being made to feel completely wrong and asocial.)

Within every family both big and little decisions have to be made. We can, without any difficulty, leave many of the little decisions to the adult who is in the middle of it all and let them sort it all out. Perhaps the decision needs to be debated afterwards. Nevertheless, the adults must make the big decisions together—and with the children if they are more than four or five years old and the decision has significant consequences for their lives. For example:

Where should the kids go to school?

Should one of the parents accept an offer of working abroad for a period of four years or more? And should the whole family move?

Should one of the adults work part-time in order to take better care of the children and family?

One of the adults wants to start a supplementary education which will take many years and cost money, time and extended periods of time away from the family.

Dad wants to have more children, but his partner is not so sure.

The relationship with grandma has become complicated. What should we do?

Should we take out a loan to make our dream of a beach house come true, or wait until we have the money?

Granddad has died. Should the children go to the funeral, or are they too young?

The school psychologist thinks our son might have brain damage. What should we do?

We have decided to divorce. What should we do with the children?

The most appropriate background for making such serious decisions is when everyone involved talks about themselves and for themselves. That is, tries to formulate and express their own arguments for and against, talk about their doubts, fears, dreams, visions and reservations. In other words: everything that occurs to them in relation to the issue. At the outset we do not know which thoughts we will have or how we will feel when everything is said and done. Therefore, the decision-making process must be allowed to take as long as required. A few days at least, but it could take weeks or months. That is a long time—but it is often only a fraction of the time we would otherwise spend fighting over the consequences of a decision made in haste.

It will be destructive to the process and to the quality of the answer and the solution if the parties do not observe a few basic rules: Only talk for and about yourself. No criticism of each other's thoughts, feelings or experiences. Only argue for your own thoughts—not against the other person's. The more energy we are forced to use defending our feelings and opinions, the less creative and flexible we become and the whole thing runs the risk of ending in a power struggle.

When this process is carried out constructively the result often appears all by itself. Alternatively, the couple might choose one of the original proposals without the other party feeling overruled or feeling like a loser.

One of the most wonderful qualities of equal dignity—in any kind of relationship—is that it lays the groundwork for reciprocity. Of course, reciprocity marks every family because the family is a human system that is subjected to certain systemic laws. Everyone in the system influences and is constantly influenced by the others simply by being part of the one community. This is the basic and immediate reciprocity within the family.

There is, however, also a more conscious reciprocity. The willingness to develop and learn from each other based on what happens between the various members. As parents we are able to learn from each of our children's reactions. We can learn how we most constructively are able to relate to them. That is what parents need to do with infants but often forget to continue after a couple years. It is a shame really because what could actually happen is that we start dividing our focus in two—we continue learning about the child but also learn more about ourselves.

Earlier in this book I have warned against using general methods and techniques in dealing with children. One of the most important reasons is that these either completely ignore or make it impossible for reciprocity to develop. Let us take a look at the so-called 5-minute method or control crying method which every now and then becomes a popular way of trying to get small children to fall asleep. The method involves one of the parents completing the usual "good-night routines", giving the child a loving kiss and saying "Good night. Now it's time for you to sleep!" Thereafter the parent leaves the child's bedroom. If the child is not ready to sleep and therefore protests loudly, the parents will wait for five minutes before one of them reenters the bedroom, comforts the child and says "Now it's time for you to sleep!" Then the parent leaves and waits a bit longer before reentering. This process goes on until the child is so exhausted that he or she falls asleep.

This, and many similar methods, have their roots in behavioral psychology and are totally devoid of reciprocity. It is a unilateral strategy that the adults (those in power) subject the children (the powerless) to. The only thing the adults might achieve is that the child learns to fall asleep on command. It is a method which is not at all concerned with the character of reciprocal relations within the family, the parents' values or the child's personal integrity. It has, as such, nothing to do with upbringing or interaction—instead it is a kind of training. The fact is that training actually works with children if the adults are consistent, goal-oriented and they persevere. Thousands of parents have tried this method—many should be complimented for having given up halfway.

The alternative to methods like this is to look more closely at oneself, the child and if anything at that particular point in time marks the mutual relationship. Let us look at a couple of examples:

I met with a young mother who had a two year old girl. She had mentioned that she wanted to talk about what she called "our daughter's sleep problems". As it turned out, we didn't have time for a thorough talk about this but had to make do with five minutes. The situation was classic—one of the parents put the child to bed at a time which took her sleep needs into account but it took three to four hours before she finally fell asleep, and then often on the sofa in the living room between the parents.

During our conversation I had the impression that it was a typical modern family which was completely focused on their role as parents. They were very focused on all the child's wishes and needs and tried as hard as possible to avoid conflicts. A bit à la "This is not just a child. It is the beginning of a new and better humankind."

I therefore suggested to the mother that she and her husband spoke about what was most important for them to pass on to their daughter. A couple weeks later she called and said:

"The situation is such that my mother was mentally ill and died when I was 10 years old. I didn't get a chance to have much contact with her. My husband lost his father when he was four. We had never really spoken about it before, but now we worked out that the most important thing for us is that our daughter gets as much contact and care as possible. When we were able to formulate that we suddenly saw that it was a rather a self-centered project that didn't leave much room for our daughter. Neither did it leave room for who she is and what she wants. Since our conversation she falls asleep shortly after we've tucked her in and said good night!"

Because these parents did not use a method, they learned something important about themselves and in relation to their daughter, which is, in fact, quite valid for everyone:

As parents, we have to try to curb our own self-centeredness—our single-minded focus on whether we are good enough as parents—and learn that gifts are exchanged in both directions.

It is always dangerous to turn one's child into one's "project" because it erases the child's individuality and thereby their equal dignity. In this case one can say that the project was similar to every parent's project, namely to give their own children a better childhood than they had. It is a beautiful and often also necessary ambition but too often the child's own needs, limits and goals disappear from sight.

So called sleep problems, like so many other "problems", are very seldom the actual problem. They are warnings, which should draw the attention to the fact that something in the mutual relationship needs to be adjusted.

Young children (as well as older ones) have their own limits for how much intense attention they can take without becoming stressed, troubled or desperate.

A different couple spoke to me at great length and detail about their nine month old son's problems with falling asleep. They tucked him in using all the tricks of the trade but it could still take up to an hour before he actually fell asleep and then only if one of the parents sat and held his hand. The parents were so serious and worried that I thought it was a bit out of proportion. I told them this and encouraged them to relax. The mother got a little offended and said "Yes, but we can't just do that. Imagine if he has a problem!"

It turned out that the mother's oldest sister had a child who found it very difficult to fall asleep. This was partly because of a rare intestinal infection which induced great pain. Therefore, it was important for this mother that her son was able to fall asleep quickly—it did in fact cause her a great deal of anxiety. Falling asleep quickly was the same as being healthy.

After some time the parents were able to separate their own child and the sister-in-law's child in their consciousness. They were also able to suppress their worries, and their son was able to attend to his own sleep needs instead of his parents' anxiety.

People are different—even though we once in awhile develop symptoms that resemble those of others. The difference means that it always takes something different to clear up and solve conflicts—but only if we choose to value qualities such as equal dignity, personal integrity and reciprocity.

One of the things we all have in common is our deep and continuous need to experience that we are of value to the people we love. It is one of life's many paradoxes that this need makes us extremely self-centered. Not self-centered understood as a moral condemnation. Instead, we become absorbed in ourselves, what we can do and what we would like to give. We focus on doing the right thing, not making mistakes, being enough for each other and so forth.

The only real antidote to self-centeredness is our willingness to be open, curious and interested in the other party. We must be willing to explore whether everything we are doing in order to have value for the other party is, in fact, also experienced as being valuable by the other party. Historically speaking, we have developed two different reactions when this turns out not to be the case.

If we're talking about children, we often react by doing more of the same. Who has not heard themselves say "I don't know how many times I've said it to him, but it's not working!" In that case it is safe to assume that we have been saying the wrong things. Children often have an unmistakable and cunning ability to subconsciously put their finger on their parents' sorest points—the inner and outer behavior I called self-destructive in the beginning of this chapter, which in love-based relationships also always becomes destructive for everybody else. It means that they can play a very concrete, inspirational and helpful role in the parents' personal development process. It is a wise move to accept that gift. Both for the sake of oneself, of course, but also for the sake of building a relationship based on equal dignity where everyone's values are acknowledged and the children are not just symbols of their parents' success. Put in an historical perspective, this phenomenon has been perceived as though children were provoking and needed to be changed. Children actually have to be relatively old before they consciously try to provoke their parents. It is certainly true that parents often feel provoked but that is something entirely different. There is no reasonable justification to blame children for that. It belongs to the category of feelings that we need take care of ourselves.

In relation to our adult partners, we are inclined to interpret it as a rejection when our well-intentioned gifts are not well-received—or even returned. We take it personally instead of learning from it. Try to notice next time you have had a conflict with your partner and go around and brood about it. Most likely, the lion's share of your thoughts has to do with justifying yourself or finding mistakes and weaknesses in your partner. This is pure self-centeredness of the unfruitful kind. Constructive self-centeredness asks this question:

> "How could I possibly have said what was on my mind in such a way that it could have enriched our relationship and made me a more authentic person?"

The first form of self-centeredness is just a wreckage from our own upbringing when we took our parents' mistakes and offenses and saw these as our faults. This is reciprocity's enemy no. 1 and will inevitably end in loneliness.

I don't think it is possible to live together as a family without having power struggles left, right and center—over the first

10-15 years in any case. That does not change the fact that they are a waste of time and energy. When and if there are too many of them, we can either attempt to win every time and thereby lose the relationship, or take a step back and seek equal dignity—not as a happy medium, but as a form of dialog where we can grow instead of relinquish integrity and community.

# Integrity

We have only recently begun to take the individual person's needs, limits and values seriously. The life and survival of the group used to be more important. Cinderella's stepsisters had to give up their integrity, cut off a toe and chop off a heel in an effort to live up to the group's ideal and get married. When my generation married we were taught the necessity of compromising and adapting ourselves. When things were pushed to the extremes there was no doubt, it was either the individual or the group/family—and more often than not, the choice fell in the group's favor. Such were the values of that era.

We are talking about a long historical period of time when the integrity of children—their physical and mental limits and needs—were systematically violated as part of the upbringing. This was considered proper and necessary. It was also the era when women's integrity was ignored or violated within the family, and when men's integrity suffered the same fate in the workplace—especially if he was a blue-collar or clerical worker.

Imagining the opposite—the individual above all—is neither possible nor desirable. We can ignore the community for a while, but we cannot avoid being part of it. To a very great extent we can choose whether or not we are going to contribute to the community with energy or drain it for energy. It is, on the other hand, both possible and desirable that families and other groups become more open and broad-minded in relation to the individual person's integrity and uniqueness. Had this indeed been a solid tradition, low self-esteem would not be such a widespread condition in many cultures and we would not have found it so embarrassingly difficult to integrate people from other cultures into our communities.

As the old saying goes "One must sacrifice one's individuality if the group is going to be strong". Since the 1970s the social/psychological work with groups of every type, as well as therapeutic work with couples and families, has taught us something different—the stronger the individual person is, the stronger the group will become. We say "The chain is only as strong as its weakest link." This certainly holds true within the family. Be aware though, it is not either/or. This does not mean that a strong individual is a prerequisite for the family. An interchange between the family and the individual does happens—the family helps strengthen the individual, who thereafter makes the family stronger. Therefore, it is in everybody's best interests to look after the individual's integrity—that it is not violated and that it has the best possible environment to advance and develop. Similarly, it is important for the whole family that the individual learns to ask him or herself:

"Is it my central needs, my personal limits or my most precious values that are at stake, or is it just a random desire, an old habit, a fixed idea or a pig-headed opinion?"

This question was perhaps easier to answer during times of material shortage when most people had to fight a lifelong battle to get their central needs fulfilled. In today's affluent society it can be difficult to make the distinction.

"If my wife wants to go part-time in order to be less stressed, I might have to give up playing tennis. Tennis is not a need, but a desire. I do have the need for exercise, but I could just as well go for an hours walk every day."

"My children want to have dinner at McDonald's Saturday evening. It is a desire they have and a way for them to meet their need for food. I am not violating their integrity by saying no. I am just frustrating their desires."

"My son wants a pair of expensive Nikes. He needs to have shoes on his feet but he does not need Nike shoes. Maybe it is a social need because some other kids have them but I am not violating his integrity by buying something less expensive."

"I am married for the second time to a woman who has two young children. I think her way of raising them is completely hopeless. I have three adult children and know what it is all about therefore I have every right to criticize her. Or, maybe I should remind myself that I might have been a father to my own children, but I have never tried being mother to her children . . . so maybe . . . ?"

We live in a state of constant and lifelong tension between integrity and cooperation. That is, on one hand our need to remain true to ourselves and to be able to develop in our own way at our own pace. On the other hand is our urge to adapt to, imitate and cooperate with the people who mean the most to us. This conflict comes into play as an existential dimension as well as the social. We can, for example, talk about the conflict between the individual and group, between the individual and society or between individuality and conformity. We do not like to be/look like everybody else—at the same time we do not like to be left out or be different. We can decide to remove this conflict by defining ourselves as outsiders or individualists, but usually we get together with others who have the same attitude and then we are back where we started—just a bit alternatively conforming!

This development can clearly be heard in the words we choose when we say "Just be yourself!" to the uncertain. "You shouldn't try to be like everybody else—just try to be yourself!" say the reflective young people who are in the midst of a crisis. "You can't satisfy everybody, so what's important is being true to yourself!" say the middle-aged in the midst of their crises.

Philosophy and psychology are also concerned with the self so just what is it really and where do you find it? The latter is much easier to answer than the former. The self sits in the brain just like thoughts, feelings, values and everything else that defines us as human beings. When we are going to answer the former question we have to resort to synonyms and talk about our real self, our true self, our core or our center but it is not very specific. We can teach ourselves to experience the difference between being in balance and being out of balance. We can learn the different experiences between acting in agreement with our self and from lying or playing a part. We can learn to be personally and authentically present when we are with other people as opposed to being artificial, pretentious or acting. We can, in other words, learn to recognize our self when we meet it, just as those who are closest to us can often sense the difference.

A woman recently expressed it this way:

> "My boyfriend talks a lot—an awful lot—but I can never really figure out who is talking. Only when I decide to pack my bags and leave will I suddenly hear him talking. I always hear him when I go, but never when I come to him. It's just so lonely!"

She expresses and encapsulates many of her fellow sisters' frustration over men's tendency to use a concrete and impersonal language rather than one which is close and personal.

So the self is an experience which changes in line with our personal and social development. From day to day this experience will change and be different. It is very much determined by the relationships we enter into. This is a highly dynamic and relational experience—not a static one.

The family is the most important place where our self and our personal integrity is developed—not just our children's, but indeed also the adults'. You certainly do not have to have a degree in philosophy to take part. The only thing which is needed is to train your ability to sense your self (your feelings) and to take note of your *self* (your thoughts and values), and then be able to reflect on what you discover. This concerns our own integrity. When it comes to our duty to care for other peoples' integrity, we are talking about our ability to feel empathy—the ability to be compassionate and to tune into others' feelings, moods, needs and limits. We learn this by living with each other and relating to our interactions. It is a learning process full of mistakes and misunderstandings interrupted by moments and periods when we feel comfortable with life as it is. Some people are so lucky to have grown up in families where they received these qualities from birth while others have had to wait until they start their own families—maybe the first, second or third time.

It is about putting together our own experience-based puzzle of genes, culture and feelings through interactions with others. The extent to which it develops uniquely (that is, quite differently from others) is apparently not important. On the other hand, it is crucial that it is personal, which means that we ourselves have reflected upon and made up our own minds well enough to stand by who we are—for better or worse. In other words; personal integrity, one of life's core values, is the sum of feelings, values and thoughts. It is about the care and respect we show ourselves and each other.

The last few years have been marked by the dangerous illusion that life can be and should be painless. It is thereforc necessary to emphasize that this mutual learning process—where we discover ourselves and each other—by definition is disharmonious and will hurt the soul many times. That is true both for adults as it is for children but it does not mean that we have to inflict pain upon each other for pedagogical purposes. We just need to realize that our way of being might at times be painful for those closest to us. When this does happen we must be willing to take personal responsibility for it.

It is this two-fold illusion which the so-called servicing parents suffer from. They think that they can make children's lives conflict-free, problem-free and pain-free. They also believe that this creates harmonious people with a harmonious relation to other people. It does not! On the contrary, it creates egocentric, antisocial children who lack empathy and become very lonely. The other illusion is that some try to be parents without inflicting any pain on their child. This is impossible. None of us are easy to live with and those who make a project out of trying will eventually end up paying the highest price of all, namely that the lies upon which their lives are based will fall apart—so will their relations. I am not trying to idealize pain—but simply remind you of its existence and legitimacy.

We most clearly discover our needs and their importance when they are not fulfilled. We are only able to define our personal limits when somebody tests them. We acknowledge the character and depth of our feelings only when we get out where we cannot touch the bottom and lose track of ourselves and our self-control. The good thing is that we get to know ourselves better, but the main advantage is perhaps that our empathy and ability to acknowledge other people's individuality will improve. (I ought to note that there are many people who have been victims of violations, disappointments and injustices during their childhood. For them it might be extremely difficult to learn more about themselves in this manner. All it might do is confirm and build on their experiences that others only have evil in mind.)

Most people can see the importance of paying attention to children's personal integrity—as long as we are not talking about deliberately violating the child physically, mentally and sexually. I shall get back to children in a moment but first a few words about the adult partners. We are dealing with their own personal limits and needs so it could be argued that it is his or her own personal problem attending to these.

The answer is "No!"—our personal integrity develops and is realized by virtue of our relationships with those we love, among other things. That is one of the reasons why we must always talk about our problem within a love-based relationship. The other reason is that it seems to be the nature of love that we quite willingly sell-out our personal integrity for the sake of our relationship with that person. We simply say "Yes!" too often to those we love. Not nearly often enough are we willing and able to say "No!"

This makes sense when we look at the relationships between young children and their parents. The children quite simply cannot cope and live acceptable lives if the parents do not frequently down-prioritize their own needs and limits. However, there are none of those advantages in the relationship between two adults. It only creates problems and must be attributed to our irrational nature and the childlike trust with which we adapted ourselves to our parents. Therefore, we must learn to curb this tendency and help each other control it as best we can. If we are not able to do that, we will be left with a growing feeling that the relationship is like a jail and that love only has to do with relinquishing one's own needs. We simply have to help each other say "No!"—even when we would rather hear a "Yes!" The children cannot help us with this. They gladly and willingly accept any old "Yes!" regardless of how half-hearted or corrupt it is. Children, however, have the same need for help to say "No!" to parents. The "No!" they would otherwise suppress—or eventually express through poor behavior and with bad conscience.

This active and unselfish care for each other's integrity is a function of equal dignity. It is the only alternative to indifference or repression. It is also valuable because we help each other become authentic and believable. In fact, we help each other become adults. At the same time, a great benefit of this mutual caring is that we eventually come to live with people the way they actually are and not just the fantasies or adventures we spoke about when it all began.

Interest, curiosity and openness are key words if we are going to practice the concept of values in relation to children as well as adults. Later, I shall get back to some thoughts about that, but here I shall merely point out that it is very conducive to the relationship if we can learn to wake up every morning pondering the following question "I wonder who my family is made up of today?"

It is an interesting paradox that we are extremely focused on noticing the slightest changes in our children's growth and development while they are little but after a few years we apparently find greater happiness and security in the belief that we unequivocally know who and how they are. Something similar is true for our partners. Unfortunately, this makes us partially deaf and blind. Someone once wrote: "We only know the front side of our children and it is like a canvas where 80% of what we see is our own projections and expectations." Be careful categorizing those closest to you—especially when giving children nicknames that may be cute or apt early in life but later on might label their self-image.

This care for children's personal integrity is quite crucial to their development as people. From birth, infants can feel their needs and limits but they are not able to fight for their needs or defend their limits. They are completely dependent upon their parents' sensitivity and empathy, not least, their parents' desire to learn as much as possible about whom they are and how they are different not just from the average child, but also from their parents' expectations, wishes and hopes. The alternative is a parenthood lived as an extremely self-absorbed process where everything has to do with being good and correct parents, and then there is very little room for the child's independent existence because he or she has been reduced to a function of the parents' image and self-image. This way of managing parenthood is unfortunately not so rare, neither in the past nor in the present.

Many wonderful books deal with young children's needs and how to care for them. In this context I shall limit myself to talking about the way we deal with their limits. Historically, it is a dark chapter—not because parents generally are mean, but because children until quite recently have been considered only partial people and it was the parents' and society's duty to turn them into real people. Today, we know that children are born with all the important human qualities and therefore also have the same sensitivities and survival capacities as adults.

Unfortunately, it is still necessary to point out that physical and mental violence is extremely damaging. It is damaging to children as well as adults regardless of the frequency or severity. The more severe and premeditated it is, the worse it obviously is. Let me also emphasize that violence not only is destructive for the child and the adult but also for their mutual relationship.

When I speak with parents for whom smacking is a normal and necessary part of raising their children I often encounter two arguments supporting their violence. The parents claim that the violence they were subjected to as children has not harmed them (and thereby overlook the fact that they, among other things, have become violent due to it.) The other argument supporting their violence is that they cannot see that the child or their mutual relationship has been damaged. The latter is true insofar as this is precisely the nature of the violent relation—it violates the child's personal integrity to such an extent that the child gives up asserting his or her individuality and thereby becomes easy and compliant to deal with. When the child does become defiant and difficult it is often explained by saying "he is simply impossible and good for nothing!" A reaction always comes in the teenage years and this will present itself as disobedience, suicide attempts, wild and self-destructive behavior, depression and so forth. If and when this happens it is ascribed to puberty and age. It is not a coincidence that the most frequently used psychiatric diagnosis among youth where violence against children is still common is adolescent crisis. The reason for the crisis is actually not the young person's adolescent age but the indifference or the violations he or she has experienced up to that point in his or her personal history—and perhaps continues to experience.

There is a cultural difference in the way children and young people react to their parents' violence against them. In cultures where violence is common the children consciously become less critical of their parents, and they will have less resistance against using violence when they become parents themselves. Children's general conclusion regarding violence is that they are the ones who are wrong. This assumption is naturally strengthened when they can see or perceive that most adults do it against most children.

Children cooperate either straightforwardly or in an inverted way, and approximately half of the children who are victims of violence in the course of their childhood become themselves aggressive, destructive and violent as adults. The other half, who cooperate in an inverted way, direct the violence inside and become self-destructive (get married to violent men, become depressed and suicidal, become addicts and so forth). In many parts of the world it is still so that most boys become destructive and most girls self-destructive, but it is a difference that is gradually balancing out. What both sexes have in common is that they have very low feelings of self-worth and a frequent occurrence of learning problems and psycho-social difficulties.

Fortunately, our general ability to repress pain and trauma is strong, so let me close this theme by drawing attention to the fact that as a community we consider it necessary to offer psychological crisis help as quickly as possible when adults are suddenly subjected to completely unmotivated violence—and rightly so. If not, there is a great risk that they will suffer from a post-traumatic stress disorder (which among other things leads to an inability to concentrate, mood swings, difficulty sleeping, depression and so forth).

However 99% of the children who are victims of violence in the family are cut off from this kind of help and must try to survive on their own as best they can. Often they must do this with very little sympathy and understanding from the rest of their network such as preschools, school and other institutions. For these children violence is not only unexpected and unmotivated, it also comes from the people they love the most and implicitly trust. It is indeed incredible that children have this ability to survive relationships that would break most adults. This really ought to make us extremely cautious when assuming that so-called well-functioning children are doing well.

The consequences are similar when it comes to violence in love-based relationships between adults. Not simply because we perceive violence as morally wrong, but also because it draws attention to a relationship where one is lacking respect and care for the other person's integrity. This lack of care and respect always goes both ways, even when only one partner reacts verbally or physically violently. These relationships should either be dissolved or receive prompt and long-lasting help from a family therapist. It will never get better "with time"—not even a whole lot of love will help.

One of the most frequently occurring violations of children's integrity is what we call scolding or, as a five year old called it "when the grown-ups hit with the tongue". For adults to violate children's integrity in this manner is an ancient tradition with the purpose of turning them into real, proper people. The current generation of grandparents tried to change this by speaking nicely or sweetly to children which in practice meant that they said the same thing parents always have said, but in an emotionally neutral tone of voice with a tendency toward the ingratiating.

The Danish child researcher Erik Sigsgaard and his team surprised and stunned educators and parents alike when he, in a study among preschool children aged three to six, discovered that the majority of them experienced that they were scolded most of the time when they were with adults. The adults in the study did not experience that they scolded nearly as much as the children experienced that they were scolded. The important question is therefore, what happens? The quick answer is that adults use language in a way which makes children feel dumb and wrong. This hurts them deep-down and makes them sad. For example:

"It's like hitting with the tongue." (Five year old preschooler)

"They get mad about almost everything. Like when you're playing Gameboy and don't get up." (Eight year old)

"The worst thing is when the teacher gets mad. Then you don't want to be in the classroom at all." (Seven year old)

"I don't feel good. I get mad at them. I feel like leaving school and going out and playing war." (Eight year old)

The above quotes come from Erik Sigsgaard's book "Skældud" ("Scolding"/Hans Reitzels Publishing House).

Confronted with this, many parents ask "Yes, but what are we supposed to do if we're not allowed to scold?" The question is answered in one of my earlier books ("Her er jeg! Hvem er du?—om nærvær, respekt og grænser mellem børn og voksne"—"Here I am! Who are you? Resolving conflicts between adults and children" (This is a book about closeness, respect and the boundaries between adults and children.")

In this book I simply want to draw attention to some recent brain research which focuses on the brain's requirements for an ideal learning environment. This research establishes as a fact that the ability to learn is significantly reduced in an environment marked by criticism. Through clinical work focusing on children's relationships with adults it has been known for many years that this also pertains to our ability to learn social skills. Therefore scolding is not only ethically problematical but a direct contradiction—by scolding we achieve the opposite of what we aim for.

When it comes to children's abilities to learn intellectual and practical skills, a popular alternative to criticism has been positive reinforcement—a kind of fact-based praise. In ordinary child raising something similar has been attempted with varying degrees of success. In the long term it creates very uncertain and dependent people who are only able to thrive in more or less artificial environments where a number of clearly defined authoritarian figures decide what is worthy of praise and what is not.

The best alternative to scolding at home is not praise but authentic and genuine feedback. It requires conversation, dialog and negotiation for a family to function and for the various members to respect each other with equal dignity. This is the alternative to "Shhh, the adults are talking!" and "Children should be seen—not heard!" but it does require both time and energy, especially for what I call the patchwork family, where two different cultures either have to merge or figure out how to co-exist relatively peacefully. Mutual love always exists in the nuclear family and between the single parent and his or her children. This creates trust and functions as an emotional buffer between children and adults. That is not necessarily a prerequisite in the patchwork family between me and your children or yours and mine—or between the children themselves. Therefore more time, more words, greater openness and flexibility is required. Not until the children dare to trust the adults' ability and willingness to practice equal dignity can both parties begin to relax. A clear indication telling us that the adults fail to practice this important value is when the children establish a tyranny of equality, where every single good thing has to be carefully weighed before it is distributed. The exhausting pursuit of fairness with every little thing is also a sign that equal dignity needs a boost. The same is true for many other human communities—also those where only adults are involved. If not even the smallest level of equal dignity can be found then everybody will try to look out for themselves, and we end up living according to the simplified values of the market.

# Authenticity

The demand for authenticity within the family marks a quantum leap of change. It has, more than anything else since the 1990s, put parents in a difficult situation because they grew up in families where the opposite of authenticity was what was valued. Now they find themselves in relationships and have children who reject that and more or less directly insist on their parent's authentic closeness.

When I grew up, the absolute central idea of values when raising children was that children should learn to behave themselves. Linguistically, it was to be taken quite literally. It had to do with learning to act just as in a play. Children had to learn the right lines—politely say "May I please be excused?" after a meal; "Hello!"; "Thank you for the Christmas present!" and so on. When the children had learned their lines by rote and could say them at the right times, they were well-behaved—and a credit to their parents. A similar form of role-playing took place between parents, at school and in the workplace. Those were the days when the world still added up—at least from a values-related point of view.

There are many reasons for the total change in values which has recently occurred. In the context of the family, there is little doubt that women's liberation has played an important part. Some of the female traits have always been closeness and emotions—maybe because they were forced into this as the men's daily routines were outside of the family and they worked in places where closeness and feelings had a very low priority. Women are like fish in water when they can exchange feelings and experiences while many men find it difficult to see the point of this and feel like bulls in a china shop when they do attempt.

Authenticity, which essentially means genuine—the ability to express oneself credibly—is a prerequisite for three essential factors within the family:

1: For close and warm contact between adults, and between adults and children.

In this context it is important to remember that two kinds of warmth exist between people—the heat of fusion (harmony) and the heat of friction (conflict). Both are equally warm and equally conducive to growth and development, but we traditionally prefer the heat of fusion. Nevertheless, we would serve ourselves and our family best by putting them on equal footing. Conflict-free community between people of equal dignity is an illusion. Both kinds of warmth require closeness, openness and credibility.

2: For the development of personal authority and thereby the possibility of fulfilling one's needs, limits and values.

We are responsible for ourselves, and not until we master that responsibility with reasonable competence are we ready to actively enter into sharing responsibility for other people and the things we have in common with them. When raising children, this is the only alternative, based on equal dignity, to the use of violence, threats, promises and degrading manipulation. In relationships between adults it is a prerequisite for equal dignity and the only alternative to suffering as victims of other people's actions.

3: For working through and perhaps solving conflicts and problems within the family.

A useable solution cannot be found until both parties or every member of the family has expressed themselves as authentically as possible about a problem or a conflict, the way in which it affects them and their options for contributing. Otherwise, the solution will simply be a new rule or sanction.

In addition to this, there is an important quality about authenticity which is worth remembering, namely that we cannot change painful and inappropriate aspects of our inner self or behavior until we are able to express ourselves authentically—with accurate words and feelings. It is not enough to talk about ourselves if we are to develop. We have to be able to express ourselves personally and authentically—and preferably verbally—to another person who is able to listen. I write "preferably verbally" knowing that powerful, authentic expression can be found in music, theater, art and literature. The degree to which these expressions are potent enough to seriously change the nature of the artist's personal relations, I do not know. However, all artistic expressions have one thing in common, namely that they are consciously aware of the significance of authenticity. For example, the difference between playing music and simply playing the notes—music consists of the notes plus the musician's authentic and personal expression. Artistic expression also means that many people have, despite having difficulties putting words to their existence, an authenticity that continually shines through. The music plays beautifully and attentively when we are able to ignore the words or the lack of words. Those who are able to do this are everywhere—the deaf, infants, mentally handicapped and all of those who only managed to learn to talk, discuss and analyze but never learn to express themselves.

We are slowly beginning to understand the importance of authenticity in love-based relationships between adults. Perhaps we are not particularly well-skilled yet but at least we have become aware of the importance which is a really good start. Unfortunately it is a different matter all together when it comes to the way in which adults relate to children.

The authentic relation—a relationship between two people who attempt to and occasionally succeed in being authentic—is the modern alternative to previous generations' role-playing. However, it would appear that many parents still feel obliged to act like parents—that is, behave in a way which they imagine must be the "right" way. Many parents feel they are supposed to live up to the many demands which are placed on parental roles. This is evident when parents enter their social life accompanied by their children. It is, in fact, similar to what happens on the home front—just in a less polished version.

The son sits on his father's lap near the family's large round coffee table. At some point the son slides off dad's lap and tries to walk around the table. He is at that age when he cannot walk by himself yet, but the table has just the right height for him to hold onto so he can walk all the way around without further help. It means, however, that he has to hold his head over the table with his chin alarmingly close to the tabletop. After one and a half times round, the unavoidable happens—his small legs give way under him and he hits his chin on the table, he bites his lip, it bleeds and he starts to cry.

His father clearly becomes uncertain but quickly takes on the role and says with a laugh:

"You're so silly. You shouldn't have done that!"

After that he picks up his son and comforts him. If this father had expressed himself authentically he might have said something along the lines of:

"Ouch, darn it! I'm sorry—I should have taken better care of you."

Or simply empathetic:

"Ouch, that hurt, huh? And it was going so well."

There is no doubt that the two latter statements are present in his consciousness but he chooses the classic parental role where the adult plays the responsible and know-all and at the same time puts blame on the child. Not only is it a violation of the child's personal integrity (guilt and shame are the two most self-destructive emotions we know) but it also works as a serious obstacle for the son's learning process if repeated frequently. Children learn by playing—or to be more precise, adults have agreed to call children's learning and exploration play—and if learning becomes associated with guilt, it becomes difficult to learn because the child feels dumb and wrong.

In this case the child was hurt twice—first on the table and then by his father. The former is in no way harmful for his well-being and development. It is just a useful experience of what his body can and cannot do. The latter affects the quality of their mutual relationship—when one party in a relationship is concerned with emphasizing his or her own infallibility, the other party will always be left with the short straw.

When a similar situation occurs between two adults, the one with the short straw has the possibility of protesting or withdrawing from the relationship. In the relationship between parents and children, the children will learn to look up to their all-knowing parents and down upon themselves.

There are signs that we might be headed towards a new trend where parents want to be perfect in their role as parents.

This ambition of being perfect parents, which is a well-known historical phenomenon, is perhaps the very heaviest burden we can place on our children's shoulders—far heavier than the burden of having alcoholic or mentally ill parents. This is simply because the search for perfection is meaningless. Children of alcoholics have to bear a lot of responsibility and a great deal of guilt. They "grow-up too soon" as we say. Nevertheless, an overly responsible child fills a void in the family and thereby has concrete value to those closest to him or her. (They fill the responsibility which the alcoholic or the mentally ill person cannot manage to take on him or herself.)

With parents who try to be perfect, the child is reduced to a function in the parents' lives—namely to be the daily, living proof of their success, comparable with their garden, kitchen or interior design. The irresponsible father or mother actually needs a child who can carry the responsibility whereas the ambition of being a perfect parent is nothing other than a misguided, self-absorbed, neurotic idea, which others must pay the price for. Meanwhile, the perfectionist either bathes in his or her success or frets about the fiascos. All forms of perfectionism are ultimately destructive for the person who suffers from them, and not least for his or her relationships with others. It is quite simply one of the most self-destructive psychological phenomena. We know precisely what will happen in these families. About half of the children will cooperate in a straightforward way and do everything they can to live up to their parents' expectations. The other half will cooperate in an inverted way and will fight against the expectations tooth and nail. Both groups will leave childhood with very low self-worth and a thick psychological journal from school.

Listen instead to the last century's great child psychologist Bruno Bettelheim who coined the expression "A good enough parent". This notion serves children and parents much better as it leaves plenty of space for being human—for better or worse. Thereby they can, in fact, be as authentic as possible.

Parents play the roles of mother and father all the time. Most are not aware of it yet any observer can easily hear and see how they interact differently with children and other adults. Children have no automatic respect for role-conditional authorities—neither do adults for that matter. When we are talking about children over the age of four or five, parents achieve very little when they try to be pedagogues or teachers. It will last only a couple months before the children start to challenge their roles in the hope of finding a real person behind the mask. Parents actually get a long leash. Children trust their parents unconditionally and think all the way up until age nine or ten that they have the world's best parents. After that, parents quickly lose any real contact with their children if they cannot offer anything else besides role playing. Adults are no different really! We do not want to spend time and energy with other adults who only have a social role to offer, regardless of whether they play sex kitten, Tarzan, meek gray mouse or the know-all man of the world. We can put up with it and take part of their games for short periods of time, but try living with one . . . !

Becoming a parent is undeniably a new role for anyone. The question is what can new parents do to avoid behaving like actors? Here are a few things:

1: Get feedback from your partner and your friends.

2: Examine your own values and your child's needs and learn what is necessary through interaction with the child—not from people in the media who claim that everything is smooth sailing and that parenthood is the most delightful and enchanting thing that has ever happened to them. They do not represent real life parents—they are part of the editor's feel-good concept.

3: Be the best parent you can be and take responsibility for your mistakes and blunders as you discover them. You will be a better parent and your child will not be left with a sense of guilt.

4: If you are in doubt and do not get feedback from others, record yourself on a cassette or videotape for a couple hours. When you watch or listen to the tape later you will very clearly be able to see and hear when you are authentic or trying to be so, and when you are just acting.

5: Last but not least, the best thing you can do for your children is to take good care of your relationship as a couple (your adult life if you are single)! It is the most effective remedy against drowning in the role as a parent. It will be too much for the children if they are those who mean everything to their parents. That is too big a burden. Their lives and welfare are obviously hugely important to us, but to appoint the children as the meaning of my life is not healthy for any of the parties or the relationship between them.

Over the years I have met thousands of parents who were frustrated that their attempts at upbringing did not go as expected. Very often my help has consisted of leading one or both parents to finding a more authentic contact with the child they had the most conflicts with. Time and again it has surprised me as well as the parents how many of these conflicts disappear like dew in the sun when the parents get hold of themselves and express themselves as personally and authentically as they are capable of.

It has, in fact, been a first-time experience for many of these parents. This is obviously a problem as well as a challenge if they do not have any previous experience being authentic.

A nine year old boy refused to go to school for almost a year unless his mother came along and sat in the classroom with him for the whole day. The boy had his personal psychological reason for feeling anxious and insecure. The parents were otherwise healthy, strong people and completely competent parents but when this problem gradually developed they obviously began to doubt themselves. They feared that he would feel rejected and alone with his anxiety so they had chosen to give in to his wishes. They had consulted different professionals, all of whom had ideas about what they should do to change the boy's behavior, but thus far nothing had helped. At this stage the mother was in the concrete dilemma—her employer was losing patience and therefore she had to choose whether she wanted to go back to work or stay in the classroom and lose her job. I kindly challenged the mother with the following question:

—What are you going to do?

Mother: Well, I'd rather he could be at school without me.

—OK, but what are you going to do?

Mother: Well, of course I'd rather go back to work.

—Now I know what you want, but what are you going to do?

Mother: But I don't want him to think that I'm deserting him if he really needs me.

—Fine, but what are you going to do, now that you have to choose?

We continued in a similar vein for a bit, until the mother's face suddenly got red and she said:

> Mother: Now I know what it is you're asking. I simply can't answer right now. I need more time.
> —Fine, you've got all the time you need.

Two months later we had another conversation, where the mother relayed the following:

> Mother: A few days after I spoke with you, I woke up one morning and just knew that I wanted to go back to work the following Monday. I told Frederick. Of course he was very unhappy, but I stuck my ground and then went to school with him for the last time. The next morning he was both unhappy and furious and called me the world's worst mother, but I stuck to my decision to go back to work and wasn't coming to school with him. He stayed home from school for three days. Just sat in his room and was angry but then he went to school and has continued doing so ever since.

Everybody had tried to change Frederick, but it was (as always) within the parents that the change needed to take place. In this instance, first and foremost in the mother who was the primary supplier of the caring which Frederick thought that he needed. The mother had to find herself—her authentic self. When she found it, the problem disappeared. Her and Frederick's life together had always been relatively smooth and without problems. She had done well and was comfortable with just being "a good mother". She was not challenged until Frederick became anxious and fearful. She had to find herself in the role as mother.

The explanation is simple. Children have, as I shall focus on in Chapter 6, a need for their parents' leadership. Children need parents to function as a kind of lighthouse which sends out regular and clear signals so that the children can learn to navigate their life's journey. This is also how Frederick's life had been until a number of intense events made him anxious and fearful—and his parents uncertain. The parents did not have the necessary knowledge or experience to help him with his anxiety. Neither did the school psychologist, so Frederick had to come up with the medicine that he thought was best. He became the family's lighthouse. Neither children nor adults thrive when that happens. Children do not know what they need, they only know what they want. So when children's desires become the parents' guiding principle, children will not get what they need.

In order for the parents to rebuild themselves as the lighthouse in Frederick's family, the mother had some soul searching to do. Different pedagogical attempts and other tricks to motivate Frederick to attend school on his own had not worked. He needed the real thing and his own genuine fury in order to feel secure enough. One of the greatest benefits of authenticity is not just that you will know how to get a handle on yourself—others will also know how to get a handle on you.

In all families there are hours, days and longer periods where one of the members cannot be attentive and completely "there". We might simply be occupied with other things such as work, other relations, critical phases of life, meditative doubt about who we are or what we really want or a range of other things. Authentic absence one could call it, assuming of course that we are not pretending to be attentive and thus lying about it. In any case, questions arise "Who am I right now as part of this relationship? Are the thoughts I am thinking about myself also the truth about myself?" The answer is that it takes a decade or so to figure that out—at least if you are under 35 years of age and the relationship with your partner is less than 10-15 years old. We do not find the answer in isolated meditation but through interaction with others—through closeness, interplay, dialog and reflection.

A number of the patterns of our reactions and feelings are authentic. Others are "not me" patterns which we have developed in order to get through childhood as unscathed as possible.

For example, if I constantly need confirmation that I am good enough, this is not me. It has been inflicted upon me by my parents who either constantly criticized me or made me so dependent upon praise that I became afraid of the least bit of criticism. If I constantly suffer from feelings of guilt and take on the responsibility for everything between heaven and earth, it is an expression of not me. Children are not born with feelings of guilt. These feelings of guilt have been inflicted upon me by my parents who were either incapable of taking responsibility for themselves or who constantly saw me as a burden to them. If I am constantly aggressive and blow up in relation to those close to me, it is not me. This form of spontaneous, uncontrollable aggression is the twin of feeling guilty. It stems from being made to feel wrong and violated throughout my childhood or from having grown up with parents who constantly were passive and evasive so I had to be rude in order to provoke any reaction from them.

The above reflects a series of general experiences from adult psychotherapy. We must remember that countless variations can be found. We need to be open and sense our way forward, experiment, let ourselves be affected by others, listen to them and keep trying. Until suddenly the authentic expression comes to us. When it happens, we are not in doubt. Once the right words and feelings are expressed and accepted by the other party, the first reaction will be very moving. We might smile broadly and warmly to ourselves. Thereafter, a completely new sense of peace will descend—one that says "Yes, that's me—and it's OK!"

Children are authentic, until they have absorbed a certain dose of upbringing and are influenced by cultural issues. Then they enter puberty and the first conscious searching for "myself" begins. Every time we enter into a new love affair or hit an existential crisis, a new search begins. Luckily, we do not have to start all over each time.

This does not mean that we as parents are unable to support our children in their search for authenticity—to develop a healthy self-worth, as we call it. The best way of doing this is by being interested in who they are on a daily basis, by helping them express themselves authentically and not least by being as authentic as possible in our contact with them.

In our search for authenticity we must, among other things, constantly find and redefine our own limits because they change over time. They also adjust in relation to the people we are with. Children are, as mentioned, most at ease when their parents are as authentic as possible. Understandably, this makes parents nervous because the need to set limits constantly arises. Time and again this demand is also raised by pedagogues, teachers and psychologists who do not like what they call "Parents' insufficient ability to set limits". Inevitably this raises the question about which limits, when and why?

A dialog between children and adults about limits is important in relation to equal dignity, authenticity, community, leadership as well as responsibility. Therefore, I will deal with the question about limits in the following chapter.

# Responsibility

For generations responsibility and accountability have been important values for most families. The main emphasis has been on social responsibility—the responsibility we have to other people, the agreements we enter into, the promises we make, the children's well-being, their upbringing and so forth. This form of responsibility is not new and it is as important to our sense of community today as it has always been.

There is an ever increasing flexibility in terms of gender roles. This has accentuated a new dimension of social responsibility, namely, a division of the responsibility for the family's daily operation as well as the care for the children. Likewise, the increased focus on the individual person has put personal responsibility on the agenda—the responsibility each of us has for our own life, our own feelings, our actions and our choices. On occasions we also talk about existential responsibility which some call self responsibility. This term and its numerous meanings and consequences are only new to us. So new in fact that the first group of parents just now are starting to sample them as important ingredients in child raising.

Let us start by looking at this in relation to our adult lives where the results are often both uncertainty and skepticism. As personal responsibility deals with responsibility for our personal integrity, the focus is on the individual person. This means that we naturally face the fear of it negatively affecting the community and developing into a kind of individualism where everyone puts themselves first. In other words, it means that we and our children will become antisocial if we think it is important to develop personal responsibility.

For generations the family's needs have been used as an argument for limiting the individual's growth and development. Some predict that the opposite is about to happen, but there is nothing or very little in our past experience that indicates this is going to be the case. There are some people who nurse their antisocial egoism under the pretext of just being responsible for themselves by doing what they themselves feel. However, they are hardly a threat to the general society. On the contrary, all our clinical experience from therapeutic work with people indicates that the individual's well developed personal responsibility is of benefit to the community.

The interesting aspect is that laypeople have known this for several generations. Parents have taken charge of developing their children's personal responsibility as a matter of course. Mainly during the first 12 to 14 years of their lives. After that they become worried—and for good reason. Will their children develop into independent and responsible (socially responsible as well as personally responsible) adults? Many people struggle with a partner who at the age of 30 is still depending on their mother or father. Others let themselves be controlled by an earlier partner or spouse. We know that personal irresponsibility is destructive to communities but we still become a bit worried and concerned when an individual is suddenly able to assume responsibility for himself or herself. They also worry when the topic is put on the general public agenda.

Presumably, it is because the terms responsibility and power are closely related. People who are unaware of their personal responsibility or are not willing to develop it are easier to manipulate and easier to exercise control over. Paradoxically, they are also more inclined to assume power at the expense of others. We are forced to face the person who has a grip on his or her personal responsibility either with equal dignity—or not at all.

From a psychological perspective, there are two good arguments for prioritizing the development of personal responsibility in adults as well as children. The first is that personal responsibility in reality is the only alternative to becoming a victim of others. If I do not take responsibility for my personal limits and needs—my personal integrity—others will be able to treat me as they wish. Even when they do their best to treat me well, they do not know me as I know myself. If they do know me well, it is unlikely that they understand me as I understand myself. This is especially important to remember in relationships between the two genders. Men and women think, experience and express themselves so differently that it is almost a miracle that we occasionally experience—or just think we experience?—a shared understanding and feel that we are being understood by the other. Love has very little to do with this understanding even though the expression "I understand you" is often used as an expression of loving solidarity or sympathy.

The other argument is that personal responsibility is one of the most systematic phenomena we know. By systematic we mean that it largely affects the love-based relationships we enter into—regardless of whether or not we take on any responsibility at all. To the extent we do not take responsibility for ourselves as adults, it inevitably results in added responsibility for our partners. If we do not take responsibility for ourselves as parents, it inevitably results in our children taking on feelings of guilt. Whether we choose to be responsible for ourselves is not simply our problem. One way or the other, it always burdens the family. Similarly, a personally responsible individual is a benefit to the whole. Thereby, individual responsibility and personal responsibility becomes part of the prerequisite for a true social co-responsibility, which is something else and much more than self-sacrifice or charity.

Perhaps one of the most important differences between social responsibility and personal responsibility is that social responsibility to some extent can be delegated. The dirty floor does not care about who washes it, and broken appointments only reflect on the one who breaks them. Personal responsibility cannot be delegated. If I do not take responsibility for myself, then it cannot be taken by anyone else. I can try to pretend that others are responsible for me, but this is an illusion. It is practically impossible to manage another person's personal responsibility. Nevertheless, it is tempting to try, especially if a child or young person is extremely self-destructive—in the form of drug abuse, eating disorders and so forth—but it never turns out well. For shorter or longer periods of time parents can try to be useful and find an outlet for their legitimate need to feel valuable. This, however, will only be a brief respite for everyone involved because the problem with self-destructive people is in fact that they have not learned to value and take responsibility for themselves. These symptoms are also good examples of how dramatic the consequences can be for the whole family/community when the individual is not capable of taking responsibility for himself or herself—or indeed willing to so.

The expression personal responsibility as a concept might sound terribly philosophical and intangible, but it is really quite practical and straight forward.

Many modern men feel slightly defensive in relation to the women they live with. Therefore, they quite naturally often choose a defensive strategy in their way of relating to their partner's wishes and demands in the hope that they can avoid conflicts and extend conversations about feelings. They attempt (just as women were forced to a few generations ago) to be easy for the sake of domestic peace.

She: I've been thinking that we need to visit your parents soon. It's been a long time since we've seen them, and it's not right that they don't see the kids more often. What do you think?

He: Yeah . . . ? It really hasn't been that long. I don't know . . . but if you think so, let's just drive out there on Saturday.

She: Yes, but I'm asking you what you think!

He: I know, but it's not so important to me. If you think we should, we'll just drive out there.

She: I didn't say that we had to visit them . . . I asked you! We're talking about your parents, dammit!

He: Calm down. I said OK . . . ! Let's visit them on Saturday.

She: And who's going to call to make sure they're home?

He: I can do that. I'll try to remember to do it tomorrow.

This man does not take responsibility for his own personal responsibility. Consequently he does not make it clear where he stands and what he thinks. This frustrates his partner greatly because she, as a result, has to assume his responsibility for the project. In his own mind he will probably reason that it simply is not important to him whether they visit his parents or not. Thereby he has an alibi for letting her have her way. He overlooks the fact that it is important for her and for their mutual relationship that he relates responsibly to her suggestion—regardless of how important he thinks the suggestion is. As the conversation took place, she is left with a real experience of being alone with the responsibility and she is thereby lonely in their relationship. He tries to be easy out of consideration for the relationship and thereby drains it of meaning.

A similar dynamic often plays out between parents and children:

The setting is a large shopping center. A clearly Friday-tired mother is walking with a couple of shopping bags in each hand and her three year old daughter trailing a few steps behind. Suddenly the daughter sits down on the floor.

Daughter: Mahhhmeeee, I can't walk anymore!
Mother: (Turns around slowly and tries to hide her fatigue behind a bit of pedagogical optimism) Sure you can sweetie if we just walk a bit slower.

Daughter: (Lies down on the floor and raises her voice an octave) Mahhhhhhmeeeee—I can't wauuuulk. You need to carry me!

The mother considers a number of options for a moment, whereupon an expression of resignation spreads across her face and entire body. Laboriously she gathers all the bags in one hand and lifts up the daughter with the other, and they leave the shopping center.

This mother makes a defensive decision to prevent a noisy conflict. She just cannot see any other solutions. It would have been better for both, and not the least for the quality of their mutual relationship, if she had acted responsibly. For example:

Mother: Are your legs really so tired that you can't walk out?

Daughter: Yes, I just can't walk anymore!

Mother: OK. I'm also tired, and I can't carry you and all the bags. Can you stay here and take care of half of the bags while I go out with the others? Then I'll come back and get you.

Daughter: No, I want to go with you . . . !

Mother: If that's what you want, then you have to walk. I won't carry you now.

If the mother means what she says and starts to leave, the daughter will get mad at her, but she will get up and follow her. Self-responsibility is very contagious. The mother could also have chosen a different approach:

Mother: Yes, I hear that you're veeeeeeery tired! Me too. I'm so tired that I don't have the strength to carry both you and the bags, so let's lean up against this wall and rest a bit until you can walk again.

In the first example, the mother sets the stage for—or continues to build on—a relationship with the daughter where the little girl can manipulate her mother by being pitiful or difficult, which is unhealthy for both parties. The mother delivers the service demanded but at the expense of her own well-being. She sacrifices herself, and in the long run the daughter will pay a price for this lack of self-responsibility in the form of guilt feelings. The mother also pays a price, as it will become more and more difficult for her to enjoy their relationship since she will only experience it as demanding, trying and filled with many more conflicts than she had ever feared.

Some might object that the mother's strategy was, in fact, suitable considering the negative attention the conflict could have brought about in a public place with lots of people looking on. The answer to this objection is a question—Who should be responsible for the quality of their relationship? The mother or some random people in a supermarket?

The example is not about who gets their way. The daughter is not proposing a power struggle, she is just asking for the thing she wants most of all right here and now. On another day where she herself was in better shape the same mother could have done precisely what she ended up doing—carry the bags and her daughter at the same time.

If the decision had been made on the basis of her energetic and caring mood it would have been all right. However, then the daughter would not have been confronted with her mother's resignation and reluctant sacrifice.

The dynamics between people in a family are such that if someone makes defensive decisions—those that are made to avoid something—then they will always get more of what they tried to avoid. Conflicts cannot be avoided—they can only be postponed. The opposite of a defensive decision is a responsible decision.

There is a big difference between compromising and compromising oneself. From case to case we must explore where the boundaries between the two lie. If one person wants the walls in the living room painted white and another one wants them green it can be necessary for one of them to give in, or that the result becomes something else entirely which both can live with. The one who compromises has to explore internally whether it is a responsible compromise. He or she must also be careful not to add it to the list of what the other person owes (now she got her way with the green, then I can pick the tiles for the bathroom!). There is nothing wrong with giving up a need, a desire or a wish out of consideration for the community as long as we are prepared to take responsibility for having done so and do not blame others or hold them ransom. In the same way, there is nothing wrong with complying with the other person's wishes or needs if it is done responsibly.

The situation is different if one person is lacking sympathy and respect for the other's friends or family, and therefore has to choose between staying away or pretending and acting. It is also a different situation if one person wants a sexual practice that causes physical pain or in other ways violates the partner's moral conceptions. When so much is at stake each of us have to choose to be true to our own integrity. This means that we cannot demand the other person's approval—only his or her respect. To compromise your own integrity out of consideration for harmony in a love-based relationship is often a ticking bomb. As stated earlier, it can take a long time before we are able to distinguish with some degree of certainty between me and not me. Therefore, very few are able to avoid such compromises. The ticking bomb in the relationship can only be defused by taking full personal responsibility for our errors of judgment—even if we might have made them under intellectual or emotional duress from the other party.

The challenges are numerous and of very different nature:

"Will I move with my partner to his native country because he is homesick and has a better chance of getting work there?"

"Will I cancel the course I had signed up for and instead take care of the kids while my partner attends a course?"

"Will I visit my partner's best friend and her husband even though they are not really my preferred company?"

"Will I give up the relationship with my girlfriend because she does not get along with my children?"

"Will I go to church with my partner even though I don't share his religious beliefs?"

"He has hit me twice this month. Will I live with the risk of further violence?"

"My partner has been unfaithful to me. Will I continue living with her or will I break up?"

If the answer to any of these questions is "Yes!" the entire answer must be "Yes I will, and I'll take full responsibility for it!" If the answer is "Yes, but . . ." then you might not have taken enough note of how you feel or you might already have started thinking about a payback. If the answer is "No!" it is wise to give yourself time to take note of whether it honestly is the right answer which is something quite different from making a profitability analysis.

The point is that we must be responsible for ourselves. An important reason is that it always increases the quality of the relationship. The fact that it increases the quality of our own individual existence at the same time does not make it a selfish project.

The impact on a community can often be seen most clearly in relationships when someone is overtly irresponsible for themselves—for example an addict. Less obvious forms of self-destructive behaviour also have a negative impact. "Mr Nice Guy" who is always good, cooperative and helpful can also act irresponsibly and have a negative impact due to his lack of input, objections and personal point of view. A slightly paranoid person who always sees herself as a victim can have a negative impact. As can the aggressive person who explodes every now and then but always finds someone or something else to blame for his outbursts.

We need to help each other say "No!"—even to each other—and be able to feel comfortable about it. We also need to support each other to uncover what it is within ourselves which we need to take responsibility for. We need help building up the courage to be daring and do it. I write "daring" because many people grow up in families where love is equivalent to not being personally responsible. Rather, it is equivalent to always submitting to the majority, the dominating person or those to who are in power. It means that these people are lacking practice in taking personal responsibility and at the same time are afraid that it will be perceived as antisocial or inconsiderate if they do.

The latter applies to children in particular. They are quite fundamentally prepared to give up themselves for the sake of their parents' recognition, love or praise or out of fear for the consequences or punishment that might follow.

Children's first clear attempt to claim back their personal responsibility which their parents took on their behalf usually comes around the age of two. The phase we with an old-fashioned and mistaken expression call the terrible twos. At that age children suddenly want to do many things by themselves. Things their parents previously did and took responsibility for. They did everything at the right time and in the right way and for many good reasons. Nevertheless, the children can actually do many of these things themselves—and take responsibility for them. They will also try and attempt many other things and work out for themselves that they are not ready for them—yet. Children at this age do not really know their own limitations but they constantly want to do a little bit more than they are able to. This is wonderful as it is the only way for them to develop. In some cultures parents still interpret this dawning personal responsibility as a declaration of war, a blow against their power and their roles as parents. Therefore, we know that the child's desire for self-responsibility can be broken in the course of just a few months.

At the age of two the child's activities are all about trying to master daily events such as putting on shoes, brushing teeth, baking cakes and so forth. This is a form of active research in relation to everyday life and the parents' indispensability as helpers and authorities. It is also about some far more existential questions of the next determining phase, namely puberty:

"Who am I? Who do I want to be?"

"How am I similar to my parents, and how are we different?"

"Shall I find new role models and new authorities or have I had such bad experiences that I am only willing to follow my own guidance?"

Even very young children can take responsibility for themselves in certain areas but we do not yet know exactly which and when. Everything indicates that this depends on the individual and it is, of course, highly dependent on whether the parents are open and ready for this or are more self-occupied with their own usefulness as total suppliers of care and responsibility.

If we take a quick age-related cross-section of children, they can manage responsibility for their own affairs in the following areas:

From birth they can take responsibility for their own appetite and sense of taste.

They can take responsibility for the nature of their relations to adults beyond close family members.

They can learn to take responsibility for their sleep so they can be in complete charge when they start school.

When they start school they can take responsibility for their homework, their choice of friends, their appearance and clothing, the administration of their pocket money, their own food, laundry and hygiene.

They can also take responsibility for their feelings and actions.

Ordinary children can take responsibility for all this plus a whole lot more before they turn 12 years old. The prerequisite is that their parents show the right leadership. It also requires that the parents on a daily basis attempt to demonstrate personal responsibility through their interactions with each other and the children. I will get back to leadership in a later chapter. In the following we will take a closer look at adults' self-responsibility when interacting with children.

We must try to be as authentic and responsible as possible. This requires, as I touched upon earlier, that we occasionally have to say "No!" to others. Much suggests that saying "No!" to children is what we like the least. I cannot explain this phenomenon but it is easy to point out how different generations and cultures attempt to tackle this unpleasantness. Parents of the post-war era always said "No!" just in case. Their discomfort was clear because the "No!" was often unfriendly, aggressive or reproachful. They also felt they had to say it a couple of times, maybe mostly for their own sake "A no is a no. Period!" and "I shouldn't have to say no more than once!" Around the turn of the century, especially in Northern Europe, parents chose the opposite approach. They always said "Yes!" just to be on the safe side. Both strategies are equally unsuitable for everyone involved and their mutual relationship. Yesterday's children grew up knowing that they were breaching the laws of love if they asked for what they wanted. Today's children grow up with the illusion that they can demand and get whatever they want.

Post-war parents could generally either refer to their poor financial situation as the reason for saying "No!" or they could refer to the morals and values-related consensus of their society. The majority of today's parents have neither of these arguments to lean on—that is, arguments outside of themselves. The arguments which they can find within themselves they would rarely dare to trust. The latter relates to the fact that 50 years ago child raising was based 80% on morality and 20% on knowledge. Today it is actually the reverse. Our knowledge about children has simply exploded over the past 30 years because we have taken a greater interest in them than any other generation before us has. Therefore many parents quite sensibly search for knowledge and ready-made answers when they are in doubt:

"How many hours of TV should children be allowed to watch?"

"Will it harm them if they play computer games for 6-7 hours every day?"

"Do children need limits—if so, which ones?"

It is not easy to gather the knowledge required to help us answer these questions or all the other ones. We live in a world that seems to have more respect for studies than for experience. Even so, far from all studies are equally credible, and in relation to many of the questions we pose, we are simply lacking experience. Parents are therefore left seeking the support of a handful of people whom they trust—a teacher at preschool, the health nurse, a family member, a good friend, doctor or some of the many books that can be found. Based on this foundation parents have to figure out what they think and what they can vouch for. From then on they need to learn from their experiences by interacting with their children and making the necessary adjustments along the way. Today's parents are pioneers in the truest sense of the word and the "experts" often lag behind.

For some families there seems to be one particular factor that tends to get in the way of their well-being. It sets out as a goal for them but often ends up as a kind of overall value. It has to do with parents' universal desire to give their children a better childhood than they themselves experienced. The problem is not the ambition, which is both honorable and understandable. It is rather the fact that we think primitively without reflecting when we try to turn this into practice. We are inclined to think in opposites instead of alternatives. This in fact characterizes the entire debate about children, parents, child raising and education.

Many parents who were raised with lots of restrictions, bans, commands and duties reacted by trying a so-called free upbringing. This caused many parents to hesitate and they became afraid of leading and influencing children all together. The children enjoyed the freedom but missed the adults' closeness and involvement. Today's parents in Scandinavia, for example, seem to want to compensate for this lack of closeness and involvement by constantly focusing on the children. They want, at whatever cost, to make sure that their children get enough attention and love. In large parts of Eastern Europe parents primarily remember their childhood as marked by hard work and economic poverty therefore they have decided that their children should not be lacking anything in a material sense and above all, they should avoid any kind of physical labor—either as children, young people or adults.

As always, children and young people cooperate, let themselves be serviced and become extremely demanding. Apparently they cannot see that their parents must often juggle several jobs or go into great debt to be able to satisfy their demands. The problem is that the parents do not see the children as they really are. Instead they are managing a self-occupied project where they quite literally invest everything in a childhood that only makes sense in their own fantasy. They are not raising happy, harmonious children who appreciate their parents' sacrifices. They are very surprised when their children become dissatisfied and egocentric. It is simply because they constantly get what they want and not what they need.

We see families where relationships between children and adults are anything but based on equal dignity and where, instead of throwing out the patriarch's throne, it has been passed on and handed over to the children. The result of this is hurting everyone. Instead of thinking through possible alternatives they simply chose the opposite solution. Without solid values there is a great risk that the same thing will happen in a few years—but in reverse. As a reaction we might see, for example, a wave of anti-materialism. Parents will most likely not be focusing on the real problem—the materialistic object's function as a symbol of love in the relationship between parents and children. And then everything can start all over again.

There is a long tradition of "solving" conflicts between children and adults by the adults using their absolute power to very quickly deny the children's wishes and to force through their own agenda. We need to search for an alternative that is not either a democracy or a children's rule, which is simply the opposite.

Part of this question will be answered in greater detail in Chapter 6. Right now the focus will be on the impact values can have when these conflicts arise. The definition of a conflict is "a situation where two people want something different." At least 50% of the time children and parents spend together is made up of conflicts.

The most important aspect is to say "Yes!" when you mean yes and to say "No!" when that is what you mean, and when in doubt, take a moment to think things through. Is it really that simple? Yes! It really is that easy—if you know or can figure out what you mean and you are able to resist being corrupted by all kinds of secondary considerations. Such as:

> "I interpret conflicts as a sign that we have a bad relationship and do everything I can to avoid them, therefore I often say "Yes!" when I actually really should be saying "No!" to the children."

Bad idea! In a healthy family there are big and little conflicts all the time. The only thing you achieve by avoiding them is that they grow bigger and bigger and that your relationship suffers long-term damage.

> "I only have my children for two weekends every month and one week during the summer break. I want us to have a nice time together."

Bad idea for the same reason as above. You cannot compensate for the pain your divorce has caused the children neither can you compensate for your limited time together. Your children will miss your authentic and personal closeness when you are together. Thereby, they will have lost their father/mother twice.

> "We're so busy and I constantly feel guilty for having too little time for the kids."

If you really feel guilty, you have to explore whether these feelings are justified. If they are you can either change your life or take responsibility for the way it is. Feelings of guilt destroy your self-respect, prevent equal dignity and make your children feel like a burden.

"I can't handle it when my children are so unhappy."

Your children do not become unhappy by hearing you say "No!" They become frustrated which is something entirely different. Childhood is one long learning process where frustration and learning are inextricably connected. Your children need sensitive parents not sentimental ones.

"Sometimes I'd rather say "No!" but I can't always come up with a good reason for it."

It is fine to give children an explanation, but sometimes we simply do not have one. There is nothing wrong with making instinctive or intuitive decisions.

"It really is hard to say "No!" when other kids in the class are allowed to."

Imagine a document that says: "I, Matilda's mother, hereby entrust the other parents in the class with the responsibility for her upbringing." Are you ready to sign it?

"The children's father is completely irresponsible, and they get everything they want when they're with him. That's why I have to say "No!" to them."

It is not as though there is a certain quota of times you need to say "No!" Instead I would suggest that you say "Yes!" and "No!" as you see fit, and not let your ex-husband's decisions determine yours.

Do we need to say "No!" to our children at all? Both yes and no! Without any doubt children need us to say "Yes!" to them as we welcome them into our family. We must say "Yes!" to their arrival in the family, to their existence and to the experiences as well as the personal development they offer us. Do they also need us to say "No!"?

Perhaps the question is formulated incorrectly. The reality is that children need their parents' authentic closeness. They need to live with and learn from people of flesh and blood. There are still people who subscribe to a rather outdated expression about defiant children—that they are testing the limits or looking for boundaries. This always happens in relationships where the adult tries to act in ways they think parents should behave. This applies to teachers and others who are part of the child's life. It is my experience that children have a different objective—to explore whether there is a person behind the role. What they are really doing is challenging our ability and willingness to be authentic, attentive and credible.

If we are going to attempt to be authentic in relation to the people we love and have families with we have to say "No!" to them quite often. The simple and most important reason for this is because we need to say "Yes!" to ourselves and to our personal integrity. At times we have to say "No!" to others in order to keep ourselves intact, to avoid compromising ourselves and to prevent becoming their victims. By doing this we are able to maintain and strengthen equal dignity within the family. It's not just about saying "No!" but being able to say it and feel comfortable about it.

We have to learn the difference between the unkind, the loving and the irresponsible "No!"

## 1: The unkind "No!"

The one where we are looking for support, justification or an explanation outside of ourselves:

No! Because you have no right to ask me for something like that.

No! Because you've been naughty.

No! Because you pester me about it all the time.

No! Because you say "No!" to me too.

No! Because it's unreasonable.

No! Because you're too tired.

No! You heard what your teacher said.

## 2: The loving "No!"

The personal one, which does not always need to be explained:

No! Because I won't.

No! Because I'd rather do something else.

No! Because it doesn't feel right to me.

3: The irresponsible "No!"

The one when we try to soften up with promises or excuses:

No! sweetie pie, not right now—maybe later.

I'm so tired now . . . can't you play by yourself for a while?

Let me illustrate it with a typical scenario where one of the parents is sitting on the sofa and reading the newspaper. Their two year old comes romping in with a picture book under her arm and wants to be read to. Dad lowers his newspaper, looks lovingly at the little one and says "No! Sophie, I won't read to you now!" and continues reading the paper.

The same scenario 40 years ago: Dad lowers the newspaper a moment and glares sternly at the child with a look which says "Can't you see I'm reading the newspaper? You should know that one doesn't interrupt one's father in that situation!" Or the father simply ignores the child, turns his head towards the kitchen and calls his wife's name in a tone that more than implies that she has not lived up to her duty, which would be to realize the child's intentions in time to stop her, take her out to the kitchen and say "Shh, Daddy's reading the newspaper. Don't disturb him!"

A generation later parents' behavior is merely opposite. Woe to the father who prefers a newspaper over his child especially if the child's mother notices what is happening! The alternative is a personal, situation-determined "No!" or "Yes!" where the father takes his time to consider the child's wish and gives a genuine and authentic answer. It is precisely the same as making up your mind about your partner's sexual intentions or your desire to go for a walk together or watch TV instead.

The exercise consists of seeing the two year old with your inner eye and imagining her reaction. The big, innocent eyes that ask the question "Do you really mean that? Do you really mean that you prefer a stupid newspaper to your cherished and irresistible little daughter?" and hear yourself answer "Yes, my dear, right now I do." Any healthy two year old will react with something that in essence means "Stupid Daddy!" and the answer to that is "Yes, that's the way it is!" Over time, as it becomes possible for you to say "No!" and feel comfortable about it, the quality of the mutual relationship will improve (assuming, of course, that the answer is not always "No!").

The first question is if children are able to understand this kind of thing at all? No, they do not understand this but that is pretty much what children's childhoods are all about—being confronted with things they do not understand so often that they start to understand them.

The second question is about her disappointment in being rejected. It is a healthy and natural reaction and there should be both time and space for that. Not time to explain or to soothe or comfort, but time for her to express her feelings and get on with life when she is ready. As a parent it can be difficult coping with children's disappointments and tears. In the long run this is however more than compensated for by the many advantages there are to growing up in a family where it is alright to take personal responsibility. She will certainly need her personal responsibility around the age of 12 at the latest. Then she will need to, by herself, be able to say "Yes!" and "No!" to alcohol, drugs, sex, inappropriate internet chats, pornography, adults who make advances or boyfriends who cross the line. It really is important for children to learn that "No!" is a necessary part of any good relationship—whether this is in the family, with friends, at work or in a social relationship.

Sometimes the problem is our good conscience and good intentions. We often meet mothers who say "No!" and they continue saying "No!" but they experience that they are not heard or respected. The explanation usually turns out to be that their "No!" is a so-called conditional "No!" This means that they say "No!" with a little qualifying note in their voice which says "If you don't become too sad or think that I'm a bad mother!". Essentially, they say two things at once and end up as victims because their children and other adults around them only hear what they really want to hear.

As adults gradually learn to take responsibility for their own feelings, thoughts and values the balance between children's and adults' responsibilities within the family and for the family itself becomes healthier. It has been difficult for some generations of parents to see this. Their strong and sympathetic aspiration to include democratic values into their family life has in many ways drowned their own responsibility. For example, democratic values inevitably mean that children have the right to an explanation. This has resulted in many children having had their ears talked off. It has also resulted in parents who have constantly wanted harmony. In other words, they want their children to accept a "No!" and not only that, that they should also be able to see that it makes sense and preferably agree with the parents that it really was best. In practice, this resulted in many parents becoming dependent on their children's acceptance and understanding. The consequence of this is obviously that the children end up with the responsibility for the well-being of their family. This is to the detriment of everyone involved. The opposite of adult dictatorship is child dictatorship. The alternative to both is equal dignity and personal responsibility.

The fact that children are capable of taking responsibility for themselves in so many ways challenges our traditional understanding of what caring for children is all about. What is our adult responsibility? It also challenges our position of power.

Despite our ideals, the physical and mental care for our children is still primarily a feminine specialty and service. Throughout history this contribution has become so idealized and romanticized that it is bordering on sacrilege to question its quality or draw attention to some of its less flattering aspects. In the following, I will be brave and do both but I will try to do it as gently as possible.

For generations caring for children has meant looking after everything. We assumed an all-encompassing responsibility for their life as well as for their person. We told them when they were hungry and when they had had enough. We told them when they should brush their teeth, when they should sleep, get up, go to the bathroom, do homework, remember gym clothes, change underwear and so forth. We told them how they should manage their money, what to do in their spare time, who to be friends with and what was best for their present and future. We have not just introduced and guided them when something new showed up, but have made sure that the caring flowed steadily from when they were born until they moved away from home—and preferably much longer. At the same time we complained about them being dependent and irresponsible. We have worried about how it was going to work out when it was time for them to start their own families. However nobody was going to even imply that this worry was, in fact, of our own making. It might be caused by us and because of irresponsibility from our side as we have always done everything for them!

There have been, and still are to a great extent, marked differences in the way mothers care for boys and the way they care for girls. The girls are given more personal and social responsibility earlier in their lives. This means of course that the girls become more self-sufficient, more independent and more responsible, especially since they are also receiving education and working on (almost) equal terms with boys and men. In contrast, mothers still raise sons whom they themselves would hate to marry because they are dependent (upon feminine service), irresponsible and immature. The result is that girls surpass boys in nearly all areas and find it difficult to find male partners with whom they can have a relationship based on equal dignity.

In Scandinavia they have tried to equalize and even out the gender roles in child raising—but without much success. Boys also had to wash dishes, learn to knit and so forth. Girls had to do a number of traditional boy things. It was a logical attempt from a gender-political values perspective. Nevertheless, it was yet another example of wanting to rectify a problem by doing the opposite. A workable alternative would have been to support both boys and girls in developing their own personal responsibility. We can only do that if we are ready to let go of our responsibility (obviously not the general parental responsibility for them, but the aspects of their personal responsibility which we manage on their behalf). We do this most efficiently by simply expecting that children by age of 12-14 can manage their own personal hygiene, laundry and shopping, they are able to prepare food for themselves and take care of their schooling and education. If we disregard severely developmentally and functionally handicapped children, there is nothing in the nature of neither boys nor girls to stop this from being a success. The obstacles reside between the ears of the parents and—sorry—especially the mothers.

The habit of power or the desire for direct use of power still resides mostly between the ears of fathers. They are more inclined to puff out their chests and demand sanctions and consequences, while mothers use their soft voice and appeal to understanding. Power, parental responsibility and caring have been such intertwined concepts for so many generations that untangling the threads has become one of the family's most important projects.

"What is relevant care as opposed to disabling care?"

"What is necessary use of power, and when is it abuse of power?"

"Where is the line between my parental responsibility and the children's personal responsibility?"

"Where is the line between my tendency towards over-responsibility and my personal responsibility?"

"When do I use care, power and parental responsibility to meet the children's real needs?"

"When do I do these things so that I can feel useful and when do I do them out of consideration for my image as father or mother?"

We are talking about a cultural and existential legacy that we cannot simply and easily escape. The best antidote however is called personal responsibility—the ability and willingness to reflect upon our actions and sort through these in relation to what we feel is right. The consequences of these challenges can become overwhelming especially if you live in a very clear-cut culture where people have done the same things for generations and where development and innovation triggers distrust and condemnation. In today's multicultural societies, the possibilities for making our own personal decisions are almost optimal. We have lost the security of those clear-cut cultures and are left to find it within ourselves and each other. Perhaps we can also find it in the religious or spiritual beliefs or ballasts we might have. In return we have gained freedom, and with this comes responsibility.

The four values concepts we have looked at are in many ways counter-values when compared to market values. This is not because they have been designed with that intent, it is just the way it is. Consequently it has caused parents to ask whether they can practice these values within the family when they are so different from those that characterize society. Naturally, I cannot answer that question on behalf of your individual family. What I can do is point out that the values of this book reflect a view of human nature that you may or may not find important. The mere fact that it encompasses some experiences and ideas about what is good for the individual person and for the relationship between people naturally raises views contrary to a reality where people's worth is determined by their roles as sellers and consumers—respectively.

For some time a little group within the economic elite in the United States has tried to regulate the relationship between couples with the help of contracts which, among other things, determine in detail how many hours a week the couple should spend together, how often they should have sex, what would happen in the event of unwanted pregnancy and so forth. The only thing that has been achieved with this way of using business values and methods was that break-ups and divorces were conceptually changed and became breaches of contracts.

I have also met parents who have attempted to use market values in relation to their children's contribution to the family community. They have simply put a price on every duty at home—a bit of money for washing the dishes, a bit more for walking the dog and so forth. Of course their hope is that the arguments will be replaced with regulated collective bargaining tools. The ultimate aim was that family life would become a harmonious, undisturbed spare-time activity where only positive and happy feelings were permitted.

The underlying aim of both these rather extreme examples is to limit the irrational and emotional interactions between people. Those principles are very far removed from the values of this book. The emphasis of our work is creating communities that can, will and do make room for the whole person.

# Community

Relationships between people—i.e. communities—in most western cultures have changed to a degree which we perhaps have not experienced since people began to move from small family clans and country towns into the bigger cities. The role of the state used to be that of uniting people but that is undergoing a process of rapid disintegration.

Nevertheless, the family is back onto the political agenda because we do not supply enough children to satisfy the market. Before long parents in many countries will presumably be financially rewarded for child number two, three and four. Then the family becomes reduced to a publicly sponsored breeding center. Today, to a large extent, we can assume that the nuclear family and the relationships between couples still arises from a foundation of emotional choice and biological instinct. Not long ago solidarity within the nuclear family and the larger family was a social and economic necessity.

Six months of the year I live in a country where it is still common for parents, children, children-in-law and grandchildren to live in the same house or apartment. This structure has nothing to do with feelings or romance. It is pure economics. The old people own the housing and the salaries are so low and prices for rental housing so high that young people are forced to continue living at home. Nursing home vacancies are so few, inadequate and expensive that younger people are forced to take care of their parents and grandparents. Very few young couples can afford to take out expensive loans so they are able to live on their own, however, when the different generations fight like cats and dogs the young ones might be forced to move.

There is a significant difference between voluntary, self-chosen communities and forced ones, therefore, the values are also different. Not all types of families are equally voluntary for all. The divorced father whose wife fell in love with another man and who only periodically has time with the children might have a rather hard time seeing the voluntariness at first. Instead, he has to seek his personal co-responsibility for the fact that things happened as they did. Not until he is able to do that and he is able to digest this reality is he really free to establish a new community with his children. The same applies to the single mother who is left with all the responsibility when the man has run away from everything. When different families merge and your children and my children suddenly have to live together they will essentially be living with strangers—strange children and a strange man or woman. This is not exactly voluntary either—even if the adults have asked oh so many times whether it really is okay. It becomes the adults' responsibility to create a community that the others, over time, want to be part of. Something similar happens in adoptive families where the child's voluntariness does not exist at all, and the possibility of deselecting each other is only extremely rarely a reality.

A similar situation is true from a purely emotional point of view. Some couples have a wonderful time doing everything together and being together all the time. Others find it difficult to breathe after a few days and need to have time and space to themselves in order to be able to enjoy being together again and to contribute to each other's lives. Some relationships start with tempestuous infatuation and great passion, others with mutual sympathy and friendship and are established as a safeguard against loneliness. They can be found in all shapes and sizes and none of them is more united or more right than others.

The nuclear family made up of father, mother and children, is still the dominant family structure—even though it is dissolved and reestablished somewhat more frequently than before. Its community is built upon falling in love, commitment, love and will—in that order. It is the quality of the adults' relationship that sets the tone, mood and atmosphere in the family. Quality in this context does not just mean their mutual love interpreted as the harmonious heat of fusion, but also equal dignity, the mutual respect and care for each other's integrity. Importantly it also includes all the irrational, tragic, humorous and unforeseeable episodes that over time make up a family's history and culture.

Falling in love—that indefinable and uncontrollable cocktail of biology and feelings—is really a state of extreme self-absorption. When we are in love the other person fills our consciousness all the time, but the most essential part of the experience is that I feel seen, accepted and delightful when I am with the one I am in love with and who is also in love with me. Therefore I want to be with him or her as much as possible. Add to that all the wonderful things being in love does with my hormones and with me. Because of these and many other reasons we idealize the people we fall in love with and are not able to see them as they really are. An old saying goes "love is blind" but it is probably falling in love, instead, that blurs the vision.

When we individually and as a couple decide to live together as a family it requires more than a spontaneous desire. It requires a certain commitment to each other—including a willingness to also take co-responsibility for the less enjoyable and an admission that we are now in a position in relation to each other where we, in a very concrete sense, become co-responsible for each other's lives and well-being for better or worse. It does not mean that we are no longer responsible for our own lives, but that we, due to our feelings for each other, are in a position where we are able to delight, disappoint, hurt and enrich each other more than anyone else is able to.

After a few years the experience of falling in love is supplemented by or, in the best case, replaced by a love which expresses an interest in and a care for the other person's peculiarities, limits and needs. It is here we learn to turn our loving feelings into loving behavior—behavior that is also experienced by the other person as loving. If it is not, we will either separate or live together in loneliness.

It is wonderful when love plays an important part of your family life. This does not mean that conflicts do not exist, but when love is present the problems and crises might be less anxious. This is where will-power comes into the picture. As we develop a more and more realistic picture of who the person we live with really is—and who we are ourselves—we have to regularly look closely at our situation. We need to look at the other person and ourselves and make some sober-minded decisions about whether we want or do not want the relationship—even though its nature might never change. As we gradually grow older and perhaps pass through multiple relationships and families, personal responsibility and personal resolve become important factors. When a relationship is not your first you will inevitably be able to make important decisions earlier on.

When feelings, commitment and determination are part of your family's foundation, your home will be the physical framework and your values the mental framework. All the other things that are needed to build a community are then ready to be added such as shared experiences, traditions, rituals, tasks, joys, sorrows, crises and so forth.

A community where some people do all the work and others sit back and contribute nothing is not a community based on equal dignity. Adults can divide the various roles by temperament, attitude, availability and/or abilities. If this results in a traditional division where the woman has the primary responsibility for the home and the man for the finances there is, by definition, nothing suppressive or undignified about that as long as all contributions are recognized as having equal dignity within the family. This is especially important if there is an opposite division of roles.

In reality, most families live with another concept of ideals. The adults share the tasks more equally where gender roles have become somewhat flexible and overlapping. This obviously depends on the needs of the family, who has time and who is available. In fact this is more than just a concept of what is ideal. In families where both adults work outside the home, sharing the tasks is a physical and mental necessity to prevent one from breaking down under the quantity of responsibilities and duties. Thereby, we are back to the social responsibility or the mutual responsibility as many prefer to call it—the responsibility which ensures the family's daily operation, equal dignity and the individual member's experiences of being of value to the community.

The expression mutual responsibility is in fact not an accurate expression as there are very few areas of a family's life where the responsibility is truly mutual. I am not certain that this is actually possible. In most families the reality is that the adults more or less openly divvy up the different areas of responsibility amongst themselves. The frustrations and conflicts usually arise when one of the parents feel like they have too many responsibilities. This makes it important to differentiate between responsibilities and tasks.

A married woman with three children expressed her dilemma like this:

> "I am almost constantly irritated with my husband because I feel like I am the one who has all the responsibility for the children and everything else at home. When I stop to think about it I know that it's unfair because he is actually very helpful and does at least as much as I do. So not only am I constantly irritated, I also feel guilty for being irritated."

The explanation turned out to be that she actually had full responsibility for the children and the daily operation of the home while he solved a great deal of tasks. He could not really understand that she found her responsibilities so exhausting. Nevertheless, he took her exhaustion and her desire for relief seriously and solved more and more tasks. Little did it help.

The difference between having responsibility and carrying out tasks is enormous. Responsibility requires mental energy all the time while performing tasks only requires the time it takes to do them. In this family the problem was quickly solved. The man was a middle manager in a big company and had plenty of experience and desire to have responsibility. Furthermore, he had no desire to be just helpful. Consequently, it had simply never occurred to either of them to reflect on the division of the responsibilities on the home front. Perhaps this is because both were business people with highly demanding jobs. As a result the home also became a kind of job where the challenge was to do things as efficiently as possible so that they could finally have time to live. In that way, much of what is a prerequisite for the community's well-being is unfortunately reduced to a kind of non-life.

This often subconscious definition of the tasks and areas of responsibility can be dangerous for the children. If it is seen as necessary that the tasks and responsibilities have to be overcome before life can really and truly begin, then the children risk seeing themselves as a hindrance and liability to the parents' life and not as an enrichment. It happens periodically in many modern families with young children. Often the children express themselves by becoming twice as demanding and difficult to be with. It is almost as if they say "If I'm only going to be a task, then I'll make sure I'm going to be the biggest and most important task of all!"

Something similar happens between adults. We can become dissatisfied without quite knowing why. The short periods of time we do have together will become disharmonious. A generally accepted explanation is that we are too busy but it really has to do with how we value the things we spend time on.

Therefore it is important that the division of the responsibilities within a family is open and transparent. In principle, it is less important whether or not the split is 50/50 but more important that the person who has responsibility for a particular area takes personal responsibility for having said "Yes!" to it. Then it is important this person gets the help, support and recognition which any responsible person needs for the responsibility to be experienced as a meaningful and a valuable contribution to the family. If that does not happen, the feeling of being taken for granted arises. This is very destructive for any community.

No family can live life preventively and therefore it is important to keep your eyes and ears open in relation to the individual family member's frustration and to sense if they are not thriving. Because the quality of the adults' relationship is so important for the whole family, it is especially important that they pay attention to each other. The ways in which you agreed to share the responsibilities and the tasks some time ago might not necessarily be those you thrive with today. It is obviously part of our personal responsibility to make the other person aware of the situation when we do not thrive but we do find it difficult to say "No!" to those closest to us. Any reproach from your partner who says "You never do anything!" really means

"I have said "Yes!" to more than feels right to me, and I would like to talk to you about that!" It is not a good idea to ignore this invitation. Not because it always results in things having to be restructured, but because you need to explore whether it is necessary to change the (im)balance. At the same time it is worth remembering that we are human beings who are irrational and often illogical (so far, it has mainly been women who have assumed this privilege, but the rest of us would do well to try more often . . !) We can very convincingly say "Yes!" to responsibilities and tasks if we want to realize some individual or joint dreams, and then a year later discover that we have said "Yes!" to too much. It is one of the many differences between love and business.

Since the 1960s the question of children's and young people's roles within the family community has been up for debate. Before the onset of World War II there were only limited choices for ordinary people. Most families were poor and had many children, while the upper classes had wet nurses and governesses. Children and young people had to help out with everything as soon as they were old enough which was at a very young age. Back then childhood was a kind of waiting room before adult life and did not hold much meaning in itself—except for the parents who needed all the help they could get.

Since then we have learned to (and can afford to) see childhood as an independent and meaningful phase of life with its own qualities and values. We have fewer children and the full-time stay-at-home housewife has become a rarity. In spite of all this, the responsibilities that come with having a family have certainly not become less. The arguments about children's roles are polarizing. One view is that it is healthy and good for children to have a certain number of chores in regards to the community. The other view is that children themselves go to work in the form of child care, preschool and school. Therefore life at home should be their haven where they can de-stress and play.

Both arguments are valid. It is without doubt important that children learn to understand that a community is not a service station but something which does demand their contribution. Whether it should happen as a gradual involvement of their natural helpfulness or in the form of structured chores is essentially a question about the parents' temperament, the family's size and the concrete need for their contribution.

At the same time it is also true that many children have very stressful daily lives. There is little doubt that simply looking at a list of chores on the refrigerator door after a long day in an institution can be what makes the battery go completely dead—or it might indeed be the straw that breaks the camel's back. It would be exactly the same for parents.

In my experience, parents should be careful not to commit themselves dogmatically to a certain model. There are so many factors at play and it might be dangerous overlooking some of these. It depends once again on the parents' fundamental values. Equal dignity demands that everyone offers his or her contribution, first and foremost in the form of their personal responsibility, and thereafter in the form of their social responsibility. Both forms of responsibility will find it difficult to grow if we continually find ourselves receiving without contributing. We lose our personal dignity which makes equal dignity impossible.

It can be very difficult to determine how children, young people and immature adults cope with the issue of receiving and contributing. They might thrive quite nicely on receiving without contributing but after a few years they will discover that they really are treating themselves poorly and lose respect for the service they receive. If the children and young people are exempt from actively contributing to the community and the parents intend this as gift of love, then the value is doubtful. This goes for the children as well as for the quality of their mutual relationship.

I have written at length about this theme in other books so here I will focus on some of the circumstances that might be why children and young people might resist contributing:

When the family community does not have much else to offer beyond a roof over the head, a bed to sleep in and a full stomach.

When the parents more or less constantly fight about the distribution of the responsibilities and tasks.

When the parents repress their children's personal responsibility, they will often react by becoming socially irresponsible.

When the parents relate to the responsibilities and chores at home as something that gets in the way of life, every happy child will stay as far away from these as they possibly can.

In general, young children's spontaneous desire and joy in helping recedes around age 10 when their relations and activities outside of the family gain greater and greater priority. This does not mean that they should get a free ticket. It just means that the parents will have to learn to tackle or ignore their whining complaints and their expressions of unfair treatment. Instead they should remind themselves that the negative feelings are not directed toward them personally but toward the tasks and chores.

The best cure for conflicts in this area is doing things together—either the whole family together or two by two. (Children do not necessarily love to vacuum, cook or do the dishes, but they love to spend time with their parents. All that is often needed is for the parents to change the way they look at the chores. If they begin to enjoy doing them, the children might start enjoying them too.) There is no point in trying to run a community of four independent businesspeople. It is more enjoyable when they all work together. Work and recreation are two sides of the same coin. If the community only comes together for recreation, the foundations erode.

The family is the place where children first and foremost learn what we call social skills, which are much more than washing dishes and cleaning up. It is here they learn about their own and others' limits as well as the importance of respecting those. They need to learn the importance of cooperation, consideration and the possibilities and limitations of the community. They also need to learn the differences between what to do within the family and outside, the informal and the formal. In very hierarchical families, the parents held the belief that children would learn those things when they were lectured to but for many reasons this is of course not so. Children learn these social values by living with adults who practice them, and the job cannot be left with the pedagogical institutions they attend.

We come from very different families and we obviously have very different experiences and interpretations of our communities. Some have been taken advantage of while others have themselves taken advantage of the community. Some have grown while others have been cut down. Some love informality and togetherness while others feel undignified or suffocated. Some have been part of the community while others have had their own and separate existence on the periphery. Some come from families which were made up of a collection of desert islands with random ferry connections while others come from families where the relations were close and nourishing at the same time.

When you start a family it is ultimately a completely new and unique adventure that never has been tried before in exactly this constellation. It is a good idea to reflect upon your own and your partner's previous experiences. We tend to choose partners who have experiences we ourselves are lacking or who are lacking experiences we ourselves have. That is a good starting point, but only if a fusion eventually occurs so both starting points are valued.

# Parental leadership

Every family will very quickly reap the benefits from trying to establish leadership based on equal dignity. It is however anything but easy. We do not have any historical precedent nor can we find role models anywhere—not in the workplace, corporate world or institutions. The ground rules of democracy will not suffice because there is a natural limit to how long the family can wait in case the voting ends in a draw. The option of using a more humorous model where the power changes hands between family members every other week is interesting but as a leadership model it is impossible. It does however very quickly give everyone an insight into the practice that hides behind the many words we often use in discussions about who is or is not right.

The equality many Northern European families experience is a result of a long, sliding tackle taken by women. They did this without encountering any substantial resistance. There are obviously many exceptions especially in families where the man still holds the legislative and the executive power. To reach leadership with equal dignity some families have been through many conversations, discussions and negotiations. Good and bad decisions have gradually allowed everyone to experience each other's competencies as well as incompetencies. They get used to being brave and laying the family's life in the hands of those who are best suited in every individual instance.

Based on my experiences so far, I believe that the most important thing we can say is that leadership with equal dignity either requires people to be grown-up or it develops them to be grown-up. By that, I mean, people who are ready to give up all of their tendencies of self-importance, self-centeredness and hunger for power. They will do this out of consideration for everybody's needs. It severely challenges people—especially those who are always cocksure, know-all and are opinionated—partly because this is hardly ever how they see themselves.

Both partners will now be aware that they can do what each of them finds most important without any serious consequences and without this necessarily being regarded as a plot against the community. The trick is to figure out what we can, want and enjoy doing together however there is not much leadership in that. Real leadership does not begin until the first child arrives. This expands and fundamentally changes the family's daily life when the family sees itself and the parents' picture of the world.

Children need adult leadership! There is absolutely no doubt about that. In families and other situations where children are forced to do without, they thrive poorly and develop poorly. The big question is of course—which kind of leadership? There is a very lively debate about that. The kind of upbringing that became common at the beginning of the last century where criticism, correction, scolding, punishment and violence were the adults' ways of dealing with conflicts or disobedience has continuously been modernized and humanized right up until today. To a certain degree it is built on outdated knowledge about children and the importance of their relations to adults, but it still has its proponents. In some countries it is dominant whilst in others it is actually reduced to a kind of nostalgia which frustrated adults tend to idealize when they think young people have become too wild and disrespectful or parents have become too lazy and irresponsible. This kind of upbringing does work especially if enough adults are in agreement that it has to work. Yet it works exclusively on the adults' terms. Nevertheless, there are still people who find it both reasonable and necessary and, moreover, consider it helpful for the children. As I have made very clear earlier on, this upbringing style builds on values and a view of human nature which I do not have much sympathy for.

One problem is that much of the debate focuses on either authoritarian upbringing or the opposite—the so-called laissez faire or free upbringing. The latter is not often practiced and is certainly not a useable alternative. In spite of this, it is as if the debate cannot get out of this outdated straitjacket. The major problem is that we tend to think in opposites instead of alternatives. I come from a field and a tradition where we look at the question from another angle—what we call the family perspective. We look at what is healthy for each individual's personal and social development and for their mutual relationship—regardless of age and gender.

We must remember that there are important differences between children and adults. One of these is that children need adult leadership but this has to be based on the same values that apply to relationships between adults.

In the early 1990s parents tried to find a form of leadership that would consider the needs of children as well as adults without violating their physical and mental integrity. Many exciting things emerged from that but also some things have proven to be less fortunate. The parents who ended up being worst off were unquestionably those who, out of sheer kindness, handed over leadership to their children. They reduced themselves to service personnel without their own visible needs, values and limits.

One value which has survived since the youth rebellion of the 1960s has to do with desire. The idealization of this concept was in effect a captivating and effective opposite to duty. The ideal freedom was associated with doing what one wanted to do. This stemmed from the reality that so many duties were associated with dislike. As a political concept it has passed its use by date a long time ago. Nonetheless, for many parents it has been important that their children should be as free as possible and be able to do what they want and get what they want. Not only that, it was also thought that saying "No!" to children's desires was the same as disregarding their needs—almost a kind of neglect.

That is in fact not at all the way things really are. Children almost always know what they want or do not want. What they do not know is anything about their overall needs. When parents use children's desires as their guide, the result is often that children do not get what they really need. One of the core needs they fail to have fulfilled is the need for their parents' leadership. On top of that, they are being fed a kind of lie about life, namely that a good life is one where they can do and get exactly what they want all the time. Reality is of course that a good life is one where we are part of meaningful relationships, one where we are of value to the communities we are part of, and one where we are reasonably free to follow our dreams and goals. This does require that we are at times forced to do things that we might not really want to do.

Spontaneous and immediate desires undeniably play a big part of our children's universes. Therefore it is no surprise that the anxiety which comes from upsetting their desires has become a kind of post-modern expression of child-friendliness and love. What has been overlooked is that children in this respect are both immature and inexperienced. This leaves their personal and social maturation process in the lurch should their desires become the governing principle. Part of the maturation process requires them to learn to pay attention to their desires, reflect upon them and decide whether they will do what they want to do:

"I want to buy those totally cool boots with my pocket money, but is that really what I am going to do?"

"I don't want to go to school today, but will I do it anyway?"

"I feel more like going to see John than washing dishes, but will I do it?"

"I want to try heroin like the others do. Will I actually do it?"

It is important that children learn to ask themselves these questions as part of the development of their personal responsibility. Part of adult leadership therefore consists of being interested in what children will do without criticizing what they want to do:

Son: Dad, I don't want to get up.
Father: OK, that's how it is sometimes—but are you going to do it anyway?
Son: But I said I don't want to!
Father: Yes, I've understood that, but what are you going to do?

It takes a few years before children learn the difference between what they will and want to do but the reward is that they thereafter can live with greater responsibility and integrity and will be better prepared to enter into relationships of equal dignity. As a significant added bonus, their self-worth is strengthened and balanced as part of the process. "But . . ." some will surely ask "if it is wrong to give children what they want, should we then stop doing it altogether?"

No, of course not. Just as you should not always deny yourself what you want. We need to do two things. The first is to add our own experiences, knowledge, values, personal integrity and responsibility to the dialog and let these be the yardsticks by which to measure our decisions.

"Now, I know what she wants, but will I also give it to her? Does it fit in with who I am, what I stand for and what I can take responsibility for, and is it important for her well-being and development?"

This means that we as parents often have to think about things before we make up our minds. Young children, in particular, find it difficult waiting for that. They just have to live with that. Once upon a time parents always had the answer right at hand, because they found most answers in their culture. It is not very often like that today. Whether the result is that the children get 20, 40 or 90% of what they want is not so important.

The other thing we have to consider is what form we will give our love and what the motivation is. If you choose the form where your say "Yes!" all the time you will get happy children, you will become very popular, and your conflicts will be few and short-lived—but only for a short while! That is what it might be like for the first three to four years. If you are really good at servicing, being self-effacing and you have enough money the harmony can probably last another couple years. But then it is over! It ends because this form of love lacks proper warmth and nourishment. Inevitably, it leads to the child becoming more and more demanding. Children have complete trust in their parents so if the parents choose this form of love, children will think that they are loved but they cannot feel it. They can warm themselves for an hour every time they get their desires fulfilled, but the rest of the time they are a bit chilly, and therefore they demand more and more of the same.

If children become spoiled it is not because they get a lot of ice cream, toys or money. It is because they get those things for the wrong reasons—the parents' seek popularity, they dread conflicts, they were met with "No!" all the time during their own childhoods or because they actually believe that this form of love is loving. It is not! It is lovingly meant but without the warmth and nourishment that is part of a relationship where the parents are authentic and personally responsible. Therefore, the relationship cannot be based on equal dignity. It is no different from adult relationships where one person constantly tries to satisfy the other and always tries to avoid conflicts. It never becomes a loving relationship.

The love we feel for our children and our partners does not in itself have any value. It has no value at all until it is converted into loving behavior—behavior that makes it possible for both to grow and develop. A great deal of that which contributes to our personal and social development is not particularly pleasurable when it happens.

We have been able to gather so much experience that we can finally formulate a list of the qualities, which adult leadership should ideally include in order for a child to experience an optimal childhood.

Below you see the qualities listed next to those that were in force a generation ago:

| Before: | Now: |
|---|---|
| Role playing | Authenticity |
| Authoritarianism | Personal authority, sparring |
| Control | Interest |
| Lecturing/punishment | Dialog/negotiation |
| Criticism/praise | Recognition |
| Power | Involvement/inclusion |

The reality of daily life is often marked by parents zig-zagging back and forth between these two sets of qualities. The starting point is mostly the good and positive but if this does not work or the children's behavior provokes the parents more than they can handle, they fall back on the tried and trusted. Sometimes these visits to the old ways of upbringing are deliberate and other times they are spontaneous or instinctive.

This practice is a natural consequence of the transitional period we live in but it undeniably makes life rather chaotic and insecure for everyone. These two sets of beliefs and behaviors stem from two sets of values which are, in principle, just as different and incompatible as oil and water. The parents will feel guilty when they take these steps back in time in order to find an escape route. For the children daily life becomes confusing at best. They have to try to navigate in relation to parents who change values more frequently than they wash hands. At worst, the parents lose credibility and the children lose their faith in the parents' competence. Precisely the same thing happens between management and employees in private and public companies when management is not able to define its values or when values and practice do not correspond.

There is an old theory which says that both parents ought to be in agreement about their children's upbringing. This demand stems from a time when every conflict between children and parents was regarded as a power struggle that the parents should and had to win. Therefore, it was important that they stuck together. Together against the children and for the demands and principles they had. In reality, it is extremely rare to meet parents who both agree about the overall values and about how they should be converted into practice. In my experience it is important, especially for the relationship between parents, that there is a certain agreement between their overall values. Preferably they also agree that the practice of these may turn out differently. Parents are different in terms of gender, temperament, personality and means and a uniform practice is neither possible nor desirable. Children are just as different as "real" people and there is no reason to think that they enjoy being treated identically or in the same way by everyone. On the contrary it is in fact a great advantage for their development that parents, daycare providers, babysitters, grandparents, aunts and uncles also act differently. There are thousands of things that determine how each of us convert our values into practice so instead of demanding fundamental uniformity of each other, it is wiser to let ourselves be inspired by each other and gradually develop a practice that is not self-contradictory.

Many families experience that one of the adults is more inclined to say "Yes!" than the other. This, in itself, is not significant. The most important thing is to explore the motives for saying "Yes!" more often than "No!" or vice versa. The motives will reveal themselves whether or not they are within the framework of the joint values. Such differences are quite common and usually arise by virtue of the dynamics between the partners. It is, for example, quite common that the one partner is more optimistic if the other is inclined to be pessimistic in their view of the world. Within a few years the pessimism of one will reinforce the optimism of the other. If the optimist falls ill or becomes unemployed and pessimistic or depressive, the other partner suddenly becomes the representative for optimism. So it is not about who we are separately, but who we are together. If a situation is so important that it requires the parents to establish something that resembles the old days' "front" it is sufficient to say "Your mother and I cannot agree on what we should say to you, and this is so important that you have to wait for an answer while we think about it some more." Perhaps you might not be nominated as "parent of the year" that particular day but that is not really so important. It is part of personal responsibility that we have to carefully consider things to maintain our self-respect rather than increase our popularity.

Another of the more problematic notions about values is that parents should be fair. I agree completely that we should try to avoid blaming children unfairly for things they have not done. The fairness which many children seek is in reality a search for equality. This is how the children might argue—if one of them gets an ice cream when she went shopping with her mother then the other should get one as well; if one child's Christmas present cost 100 dollars, then the other should cost the same; if one was given permission to go to parties when he was 12 years, four months, three days and five hours old, then the other should also be allowed at the same age. Be aware—do not jump on that bandwagon! It becomes a hellish tyranny of equality which has nothing to do with family life, community or equal dignity. The parents' duty is to treat their children as well as possible but considering children are different, they should also be treated differently. Feel free to send this message to well-meaning grandparents and others who help maintain children's illusion that absolute fairness exists. It does not! Not within the family—or any other places for that matter.

After this examination of a few old and a couple of newer values which in my experience often are more destructive than constructive, we will take a look at a new type of leadership. In other books I have analyzed and commented on a series of common and not so common conflicts between parents and their children. I have suggested ways in which parents can handle these in the best possible ways. Right now, I would like to offer a series of examples showing the importance of values in family life as well as to draw up a kind of checklist which parents can go through if they reach a dead-end. The questions that are worthwhile asking are:

"Have we actually had a dialog or have we just scolded and complained?"

"Have we acknowledged the child's starting point and reality or just tried to manipulate the way we want things done?"

"Have we taken on our responsibility and used our power or have we evaded the issue and handed over the responsibility to the children?"

"Have I actually expressed myself as authentically and personally as I can or have I just talked?"

"Was that a decision based on equal dignity or did I allow myself being talked into it?"

# Authenticity

When children come into the world they need a couple of authorities—at least. Parents who feel reasonably certain about themselves and comfortable about what they do in relation to the child. Furthermore, the parents must be capable of being attentive. This comes to most parents as a combination of information from outside and from within. They find the answers to many of the general questions in books, from nurses, mothers groups, their own mothers, doctors and others. There are many and very good reasons for taking advantage of that. It has to do with concrete knowledge and experience which used to be passed down from mother to daughter. However, these days it must be gathered from many different sources. It is different when it comes to establishing an individual and personal relationship with the child. Especially for the father who does not have an historical tradition to lean back on. Neither can he learn much from all the "experts" who by and large are women and mothers and therefore do not know much about what it means to be a father.

Children's need for an authority is a reality for their first 18-20 years of life. It is not simply about the infant's need for security but also about the older children's need for guidance and role models. They need to be able to measure themselves up against their role models. For that I consider their parents' personal authority to be most useful for everyone involved and for the quality of their mutual relationship. It is important for children and young people to be able to get a grip on their parents—to know what they think, mean and stand for as people.

Authenticity gives parents the necessary personal authority to be able to influence and make an impression on children throughout their entire childhood—an authority that parents who are not authentic but only act have for the first five to six years and definitely not when it is most needed. A father related the following example:

"When our youngest child was six or seven months old, our eldest child's jealousy came out in full force. He was only two years older and often really rough with his little sister. We tried as best we could to make him understand through common sense. We scolded him time and again and at other times we tried to make it clear to him that we were sad when he wasn't nice to the baby. None of this made any difference at all. A couple of months ago my wife was at a course for a week, so I was alone with both kids. It was a nightmare because the eldest became rougher and rougher with the baby. At one point I took him with me into the bedroom and sat down to have a serious talk. I said what I had said a thousand times before, namely that I was sad when he was mean to his sister. This time I began, to my own great surprise, to cry when I said it. He went completely quiet and stared intensely at me. He didn't say anything and when I had said my piece we just went back into the living room. It's been three months now and he hasn't treated his little sister badly even once."

A generation ago this three year old big brother would have been subjected to systematic violence, scolding or punishment until he stopped hitting his sister. The parents would not have been aware of the contradiction in their behavior—they used violence against their son in an effort to tell him that he was not allowed to do so. In those days it was considered the right thing to do for the simple reason that parents were the adults and had their good reasons. In those days parents did not realize that violence is violence, and that violence breeds violence, regardless of how it is justified.

The father cited in the example above belongs to a different era and will not use violence against his son. He believes more in conversation and reason and he is right to do so. The problem was that he just talked and talked. He was not authentically present and therefore the words did not make an impression. Words alone will not make an impression on children—or adults for that matter. There is not much in a purely intellectual way that can convince a one to five year old. Even if parents play the typical parental role with a stern face and angry voice, not much will change.

Parents are different. For some, authentic expression is softly spoken and balanced while others require the accompaniment of a small brass band. It does not matter how loud the music is but the music (the feelings) have to be there. There has to be a real person behind the words so the child can hear who is talking. That is the big prize parents have been awarded by giving up violence and threats as a means of bringing up children—and of course, the children suffer less too.

# Personal authority

Authentic feelings make up the foundation of personal authority. Often personal integrity and responsibility need to be added on top of this. In other words—the adults' care for their own needs, limits and values. These will obviously lose their impact and credibility if they do not also include care for the child's integrity. As mentioned earlier children often describe the adults' scolding as getting "hit with the tongue". They also draw attention to the disparity which exists because the adults demand respect for their limits but simultaneously violate the children's.

It is therefore the personal language and personal expression where adults define and express themselves that carry personal authority. As soon as adults start to use their power to define the child and start talking about or categorize the child, equal dignity ceases. The result is abuse of power which has a big impact on children. They react by feeling that they are wrong, they are guilty or feel ashamed, sad and/or angry. They do not develop a sense of respect, security or trust in relation to the adult authority. In spite of this, it certainly does not mean that everything adults say has to be in a considerate or diplomatic language and tone of voice. It just means that it should be heartfelt—in every sense of the word. A child's integrity is not violated by the parents' feelings. The words are those that violate, not the music.

For many years I have searched for a word or expression that could encompass the characteristic and the essence of this new parental role. For now I have settled on an expression which quite ironically stems from professional boxing. When a champion or aspiring champion has to prepare for a title match, a great deal of the training takes place with a sparring partner. This training partner gives maximal resistance and does minimal damage. Considering the fact that bringing up children has a lot to do with preparing children (training or getting them in shape) for life outside of the family, it is not a bad definition of this important part of the parental role.

The role as sparring partner is, above everything else, important for the child's ability to develop his or her personal responsibility.

Five-year-old Jonah gets an allowance and is responsible for managing the money himself. One day he says to his parents:

Jonah: I'd actually like to buy that remote control race-car we saw. On Monday I'll have enough of my own money and I'd like to buy it.

Mother: Is it something you really want, or did you just see it and thought it looked good?

Father: Jonah and I saw it at the mall yesterday. Somebody was demonstrating it outside of the toy store. It's neat.

Jonah: I really want it, and I have saved up the money.

Mother: I think you need to give it a lot of thought, Jonah, if you need to use all your money. Think about how long you've been saving!

Jonah: Yes, but it is my own money . . . ?

Mother: I'm not saying that you may not buy the car. I'm just saying that I think you should think about it—for a week, for example. Maybe it won't seem so exciting then.

Jonah (looks at his dad): May I please, Daddy?

Father: Of course you may. It's your money, but I kind of agree with your mother. It's a lot of money that you then won't have for vacation, for example. Think about it.

Jonah: OK, I'll think about it—but not for a whole week . . . !

All parties have said what they think and why and the only thing left is for Jonah to make his decision. If Jonah buys the car and later, when the family goes on vacation, regrets the purchase, the parents have to control their potential urge to say "I told you so!" That only makes Jonah feel stupid, and then he cannot learn anything from his experience. If Jonah gives into the temptation to ask for an advance on his allowance, the answer is a friendly but clear "No!"

Parents' attitudes and opinions make a big impression on children in all families even though it might not always be easy to see or hear. This is especially so in families marked by equal dignity. Jonah is only five years old and is able to accept his mother's suggestion and think it over. Not many 12 year olds can do so without feeling that they lose face. But it does not mean that the parents' recommendation has not made an impression, and ultimately he might decide to follow this.

At first glance, children and young people have a superficial or unreflective attitude towards, for example, alcohol, drugs, various norms and rules, evaluations and rules at school, etc. But if they have grown up in a family with even a reasonable amount of equal dignity they will have great respect for their parents' person. This obviously requires that the parents have not hidden themselves behind the parental role. Therefore, children will often have opinions and attitudes that are contrary to their parents' and even the most objective arguments do not make a big impression. On the other hand, it does make a big impression when it is my father or mother who says something—when it means so much to my parents as people. It often does not seem that way when it is all happening, but a reliable examination of how our values and attitudes have affected our children can be conducted when they turn 30 or start a family themselves.

Personal authority grows every time parents dare to be open, vulnerable, flexible and are willing to bear the responsibility for the quality of the family's interaction instead of blaming the children or each other. If we replace the responsibility for the quality of the family's interaction with personal responsibility, it is the same thing that creates closeness, security and reciprocity in adults' love affairs.

We often forget that childhood is a period of time when children go through enormous personal development. For this they have to let themselves be brought up (read: influenced and manipulated). On a daily basis they have to give up the inner security which they found only the day before. This is due to their biological, mental and existential dynamics. It is also out of consideration for the many expectations and demands put on them as well as their own desire to cooperate. If ordinary adults who are over 30 years of age had to live with similar demands, most would collapse from stress, have nervous break downs or suffer from frequent anxiety attacks. Children and young people need to be open, vulnerable and flexible all the time. Therefore it is a great advantage for them if their parents are also willing to. Add to this: it is the approach which fosters most equal dignity.

Children need their parents' personal authority as a kind of lighthouse. Parents regularly need to send as distinct and clear signals as possible so the children gradually are in a position where they are able to navigate and maneuver. In other words they need the space to cooperate without giving up more of themselves than necessary. At the same time I must once more warn against handing over the role of lighthouse to the children and their spontaneous wishes and desires.

It is clear that the old-fashioned philosophy of raising children with firm limits, duties, demands, consequences and punishment lives up to this need to a great degree. However, it does so at the expense of equal dignity, authenticity, reciprocity and personal responsibility and should therefore, in my opinion, be placed in a suitable museum.

Children's need for a lighthouse or two is not just about their lack of experience and the risk of running aground or being carried away by the current—their physical and mental safety. It is also very much about their need to learn how to get on with other people without this interaction always being on their own or the other people's terms. It is what we, with a modern expression, call social competence.

Meeting another person on a social level requires that both individuals are able to express who they are and what they want. It is necessary to be able to play, learn, negotiate and love and the best place to learn this is in the family because there it is manageable. Pedagogical institutions can teach children to adapt themselves to certain limits and rules and to co-operate working towards a joint goal. However, none of this will work if the children have not had the fundamental training at home.

Mother: Now I think you should put on your pajamas and brush your teeth.
Son: But I'd rather play!

Mother: Yes, I imagine so, but I want you to get ready to go to bed. Do you want help, or are you going to take care of it yourself?

Son: Ugh. I can do it myself!

The lighthouse works here, in contrast to:

Mother: Don't you think you're getting tired and that you should go to bed soon?

Son: No, I'm not tired at all, and I'm having so much fun.

Mother: But it's getting late, and you need to be well-rested for tomorrow. What do you think you're going to do at preschool tomorrow?

Son: I don't want to go to bed now!

Mother: No, I understand you'd rather play, but it's late, and you usually go to bed at around 8:00.

Son: I just want to play a little bit longer. Why can't I just play instead of that stupid old bed?

Mother: That's enough. Do as you're told, otherwise you can go to bed without a goodnight story. I don't know why we have to have all this nonsense with you every single evening when other good kids do what their parents say. Now come on over here!

In the last example the lighthouse is out of order and does not work—until the very end when the child literally collides with it. This crash is unsuitable and unfortunate in every way. The mother will presumably explain herself by saying that her child is difficult or defiant but the reality is that the child's behavior is a consequence of the mother's. At the beginning of their conversation she asks him a rhetorical question (it contains the answer itself) and tries to use a soft style. At the same time she gives her son the responsibility for reading between the lines. Naturally, he takes the lead until she strangles him. Typically, the mother really does believe that she has said to the son what she wants, but she has not done that at all. She ends up seeing herself as the victim of the son's whims because she does not take responsibility for herself.

The third alternative could be:

Mother: I think you should change to your pajamas and brush your teeth.

Son: But I'd rather play!

Mother: OK. I'd rather have you in bed so I can get my stuff done for tomorrow, and you would rather play. Give me a suggestion.

Son: I can just play until I get sleepy.

Mother: No, that's too long.

Son: OK, then just for an hour.

Mother: No. You can have 30 minutes.

Son: An hour, please!

Mother: 30 minutes. Now hurry up and play.

A lot of modern parents will take exception to the fact that the mother is the boss over the son. Is that allowed? Is this not simply the old dictatorship in a new package? Is this not a violation of her son's integrity?

Yes, it is allowed, and no, this is neither dictatorship nor a violation. Parents do frequently have to be the boss over younger children—especially if it also has to do with the parents' own needs. Gradually, there is a greater likelihood of a dialog and for a space where the two personally responsible people can meet. In the second example the mother ends up being dictatorial and abusing her power(lessness) to violate her son's personal integrity. In the first and last example the mother just gets what she wants. In the third she also gives him the option of including both of their needs in her suggestion. This is social competence at work, partly on the mother's part and partly as early practice for the son.

Personal responsibility affects the relationship regardless of whether we embrace it or not. That is the way it is in this and many similar situations of conflict between parents and children. If the parents do not take responsibility for their own needs and limits, the responsibility is passed on to the child who is just as incapable of assuming that responsibility. If the task of getting the child to bed is passed on to the other parent out of powerlessness, the child does indeed go to bed, but his and the mother's relationship continues to be destructive and joyless.

What then if the real problem is not the mother's need for him to go to bed? She might in fact think that he is actually so tired that it is best for him to go to bed. In that case the mother's role as sparring partner comes into play and then the goal is a different one entirely—namely, to teach the son to take responsibility for his own needs.

Mother: Now I think you should change to your pajamas and brush your teeth.

Son: But I'd rather play!

Mother: OK, but it looks to me like you are very tired and sleepy but are just having so much fun that you don't notice it.

Son: That's because I need to finish building the garage for the cars.

Mother: Yes, of course that's also important. But how about taking a break and checking how sleepy you are so I can figure out whether I'm completely off target?

Son: I'm not very sleepy!

Mother: I'm not convinced. To me you seem sleepy, and I think you should go to bed now.

Son: I'd rather play.

Mother: OK, then of course you should play.

Maybe the boy is in fact so sleepy that he really should choose to go to bed. However, it takes approximately a childhood for him to work that out—and even many adults cannot figure it out. At least this was the situation before we learned about the potential of children's self-responsibility. With enough conversations like the above there is no reason why the son will not be able to figure out when he needs to sleep already in the early school years. Then sleep suddenly is not about whether he is "little" and has to go to bed early or "big" and can go to bed later. Then it will be about him knowing his personal needs and limits and being able to take them into consideration if he wants to.

Children do not have any theoretical relationship with responsibility and almost never use the word. They talk about being able to decide but most of the time when they say for example "Why can't I decide for myself?" or "Why do you have to decide?" they actually mean "I'd like to have more responsibility for myself!" Because they use the word "decide" many parents feel invited to a power struggle instead of a dialog where the specific child's possibilities for taking personal responsibility in a specific area could be the joint theme.

In ideal circumstances parents can basically stop deciding, in the sense that they manage children's personal responsibility, when the children are around 10-12 years old. This does not mean that the children's need for a lighthouse is gone. Instead, their need for a lighthouse can to a greater extend be fulfilled though sparring. In the real world parents are often reluctant to resign from their management roles before it is absolutely necessary which is when the children begin to defy or ignore their decisions. If children and adolescents were able to comment on their situation they would probably quote a typical parental statement and say "I don't know how many times I've tried to say it to my parents, but if they don't want to listen, they'll have to learn the hard way!"

Children and adolescents always send a clear messages when the time comes—when they enter into what I call destructive conflicts with the parents. A destructive conflict is a conflict that is about one particular theme and repeats itself with shorter and shorter intervals. The frame of mind and the use of language becomes increasingly negative. Nine out of ten times this means that it is about time the parents give up managing the child's personal responsibility and hand it over to its rightful owner. However the need for genuine, loving and personal sparring never stops and with some luck it goes in both directions. This form of sparring is almost never misunderstood as misplaced meddling or exercise of force—unless of course it is a tactical attempt to cover up for the use of power.

Personal authority has very little to do with confidence. We do not always need to have a good grasp of our values, opinions or feelings. It is fine to stop a child or adolescent with, for example "Hey, wait a minute! I don't quite know how to explain it, but there's something about this that I don't like!" or "I'll certainly let you know what I think, but I need to think it over first!" (or talk to your mother first, your teacher, my girlfriend or whoever). We do not need to feel confident about the matter itself but simply confident that we want to figure out where we stand. Let me emphasize this is not just second best (after great personal confidence), it is in fact an excellent example of personal integrity and responsibility which children and adolescents need to rely on many times each day when they themselves have to relate to group pressure and other outside pressures. Within the family all parties benefit from children developing personal authority and personal responsibility. It makes conflicts more manageable and can especially prevent the many very big dramas that often show themselves around puberty.

Some parents have a political and philosophical resistance against exercising authority. This might be a reaction to personal violations or simply a matter of principle. It often happens with an agenda that is about keeping the culture (society's and its authorities) at bay and giving nature room. Unfortunately both parties will always end up losing. This is because parents in the children's world will have great authority. If this is obscured or kept hidden the children become uncertain and confused. In the worst case every initiative and responsibility is up to the child, and that is a crushing authoritarian demand which does not become easier to shoulder when it is placed between the lines and with anti-authoritarian kid gloves.

It is precisely this challenge adults have been trying to deal with during the course of the last 30 years. It might in fact take another generation before these practices find their natural and comfortable level. Within the individual family it can happen considerably more quickly.

# **Interest**

Collaboration with others (adults and children alike) demands that we take an interest in who they are. What do they stand for? How do they think and feel? What drives them? What are their needs and where are their limits? It might sound obvious to parents today because we are all interested in our children. The reality is, however, that we have very little tradition for turning this interest into practice. For generations it has almost exclusively been expressed in the form of questions, interviews and interrogation and even then the questions rarely have to do with who the child or young person is, but rather what they are doing.

Daycare workers will confirm that many parents ask their children the same stereotypical questions every day when they pick them up:

"Have you eaten your lunch?"

"What did you do today?"

"Have you had a good day?"

If the children were sufficiently pert at repartee, they could answer:

"Is my stomach more important to you than the rest of me?"

"I'll be sure to tell you just as soon as we've made contact with each other and if I have something important to say. I don't like making a report."

"What is a good day? And if I think that I've had a crappy day, would you still be interested—or are you just asking to reassure yourself?"

Questions are most suitable when the person asking them needs concrete information. As an expression of personal interest they have limited value and most of all they do not promote dialog based on equal dignity. The person asking can hide behind the questions while the person being asked has to be open and reveal him or herself. It is for good reasons that journalists talk about "victims" of interviews. When it has to do with building private relations and making these more nuanced, the major problem is that when we ask questions we only get answers. All we get is an answer to what we asked about. This rarely has anything to with the issues which occupies the child. The same applies to adults when we ask each other questions. After 10-12 years of asking children these questions the result is often that they simply stop answering—or answer as routinely and blankly as they are asked. As things develop the parents will naturally feel despair. Their interest is fundamentally real enough so they ask "What else am I supposed to do? If I don't ask, I never find out anything. I have to drag everything out of him!"

One or two constructive alternatives do exist. One is that the parents rigorously censor their questions and either replace the discarded ones with personal statements or do not say anything at all. The other and better alternative is to address the children with personal statements, which tell the children something about themselves. This does not mean that the parents should dump on the children but that they simply need to pull back the curtain and start talking about important and not so important events, thoughts and experiences the same way as they would to each other or to good friends. For a while that makes most people feel terribly self-centered but it is actually the opposite—you will share yourself with those closest to you. (Of course there are people who constantly chatter away about themselves, but they do not need to be cautioned against questions. They simply do not ask any.)

If we return to the parent who picks up the child at daycare let us look at an alternative to the empty routines:

"Hi Christopher! It's good to see you."

After which follows a break from talking which is used to get a sense of Christopher's mood and what he is occupied with. Then comes the practical stuff, such as concluding his activities, finding his coat and so forth. If he has not already quite voluntarily started talking about himself and his experiences by the time you are sitting in the car or standing at the bus stop, it is time to tell him something about yourself and your day. What you talk about is not important in itself but it should be important enough for you to want to share it with him. The payback quickly comes in the form of him telling you what he is thinking about, whether it is the experiences from that day or expectations about what is going to happen next weekend. Or maybe you both feel like you need silence to put the work day behind you and get closer to each other. Whatever it takes—just avoid empty routines that only serve to maintain your image of being an interested father or mother.

Children learn to speak by being spoken to and by being read to, and later they learn to read and write correctly at school. The first six to seven years they primarily learn to express themselves in the family—otherwise they will not learn to do it.

This daily updated knowledge about who the child is will obviously be important for both parties' experience of closeness and contact, but it is also an important part of the foundation for the many little and big decisions parents have to make every day on behalf of the family. This is part of their leadership function.

# Dialog and negotiation

A dialog is something different from a discussion. We are in dialog with each other to get to know more about ourselves, the other person, a subject or all three of these—not to convince the other person of what we already know or what we meant to say. In all probability children are born with the ability to participate in a dialog but they have to be stimulated and trained in order to develop that ability. Therefore it is important to involve children in as many decisions as possible. Children can be brought up to be quiet or to speak nicely but if their ability to participate in a dialog or decision-making process is going to be developed, they have to be brought in not brought up.

Many of today's families are called negotiating families often with an inference that the negotiations have gone too far. I do not think we should negotiate with children about things that in reality are not negotiable just for the sake of democracy. When parents (or children) have to make some important decisions, or have made decisions which have created significant conflict, it is time for a dialog.

When we make decisions that either concern only one of the children or the whole family we always do it with the intention that the decision should be as valuable for the individual and the community (family) as possible. Therefore it is important that we either explore ahead of time what each person sees as the most valuable, or afterwards evaluate the decision in light of the conflict it has caused.

It is not about democracy but about equal dignity. We need to talk about the issue so that everyone feels heard and taken seriously. It is not about the children's right to influence, but about the community's need for their contribution. Based on the dialog and their own life experience parents must then make the decisions they see as the most appropriate. There is no lower age limit for children's participation. The earlier they are encouraged to sit at the negotiating table the more quickly they learn to participate in a dialog and the better they appropriate the culture that is developing in the family. Before children start school they sense and highly appreciate the community's qualities but they are inclined to express themselves without a broad view of things. That comes with practice and if the parents are able to set a good example.

This form of dialog is especially important in patchwork families who do themselves a favor by having such dialogs fairly regularly which will prevent situations where families gather only when there are problems. The mood in which the adults are able to conduct the dialog is crucial for the quality of the decisions they have to make. Older children and adolescents often think they have important things to do so it can be necessary to put pressure on them to make sure they show up. The best principle is "We can talk about, debate and negotiate everything—except for the need for us to talk together".

Can a four year old really have even a slightly qualified opinion about whether it is best for her to change pre-schools? The answer is both "Yes!" and "No!" The four year old is an expert at being four years old and at being exactly who she is but she is lacking the necessary experience to make those kinds of decisions—nor should she. However the more she is heard and taken seriously in the course of the decision-making process, the easier it will be for her parents to help and support her in the transitional phase that will follow if they decide that she should be moved. Her thoughts, feelings and opinions are part of qualifying the parents as parents. The same applies to her if she as a 17 year old considers changing education or dropping out of school. It is necessary that she makes the decision herself but she preferably should not do it alone. Sparring and dialog are the only things that can ensure the quality of her decision. At the same time they are the best protection against both parties' loneliness. just as it is with adults.

# Acknowledgement and involvement

Interest in who your children are is a prerequisite for parents being able to acknowledge their opinions, feelings, dreams and goals. Not until then can parents involve or include the children in their deliberations and decisions.

Father: Aha! Now I might know what you're thinking about, Maria! It's not so much the thought of having to go to a new pre-school that you're sad about. It's because you're worried that you'd miss playing with Nicholas every day?

Maria: Yes, he's my very best friend.

Father: Yes, I can see that. It must really feel bad. I'd be sad about that too. I'm glad you said that so that we can also think about that before we decide what's going to happen.

Maria has now been seen and heard. Her father has helped her assign words to her feelings and thoughts. No matter what decision is made, the parents will be capable of looking after Maria's important relationship with Nicholas and only practical circumstances determine whether they should help her say goodbye to him or find a way in which they can still get together and play. It will be a painful loss for Maria but she does not need to bear it in loneliness. That would be the result if comfort was used instead of acknowledgement:

Father: I can understand that you think you're going to miss Nicholas, but you'll make new friends in your new preschool.

This statement is a contradictory, vague claim that either will make Maria become resigned or fight tooth and nail. Either way she will be isolated from the community with the risk of being labelled either as easy and sensible or completely hysterical.

Involvement ensures that children and young people experience that they are part of creating and forming their own reality. It is an important prerequisite for equal dignity and reciprocity. It is also a condition for children to be able to take active self-responsibility so they feel personally responsible for getting the decisions to function in practice. In addition to that, it will help them get new insights into themselves, develop their personal language and give them an experience of their existence being meaningful to their parents.

A generation ago children should be "seen but not heard!" That was then. The opposite is to let them talk all the time, regardless of the quality of what they are saying. Today we know a better alternative—acknowledgement.

# Power

In a family the adults have the power—socially, economically, physically and emotionally. Parents relate very differently to this fact. Most people in Northern Europe would rather underplay this power than overplay it. In other places adults—especially fathers—outright enjoy demonstrating their power publicly.

What is most crucial for the well-being and development of the children is the way parents choose to use their psychological and physical power. In essence it has to do with which guidelines are most appropriate. Regardless of children's genetic heredity and possible illnesses, handicaps or syndromes it is first and foremost the parents' administration of this power that determines whether children get the possibility of utilizing their personal and social potential fully. It is in many ways a terrifying power to have, and luckily, it does make many parents feel humble rather than powerful.

The only thing we parents definitely have in common is that it is not always easy for our children to live with us. They get a lot from us, sure. They certainly also lose some of themselves along the way. They develop qualities, talents and behaviors which they might not have been able to develop in another family and there is no reason to feel either guilty or proud about that.

One of the most destructive forms of power is powerlessness. It is that which most often leads to abuse of power and violations of children's personal integrity. If not it will lead to resignation, passivity and loss of contact and then we call it neglect. It is neither unusual nor dangerous to feel powerless now and then but if the feeling grows and takes up more and more of the time we spend with the children, then there is a need for help. Reciprocal pain is the motivation and the parents' personal responsibility and integrity are the road to change.

As previously mentioned, a relatively new form of neglect takes place when parents do not use their personal authority and power in relation to children but instead hand these over to the children. It is a defensive strategy by nature which in the long run creates precisely the individual and family problems one had hoped to avoid. It is often practiced by very sensitive, involved and loving parents who only rarely would cause their children harm if they just dared to assume the power and authority.

Children cannot always understand why their parents have to decide this or that. Reality is that they do not have to understand this. If the parents can administer their power just somewhat in line with the values presented in this book, children learn to feel comfort and security with their parent's position of power and that is much more important than being able to understand it or to be in agreement about the details. As parents we often make decisions that we actually cannot explain in a sensible way for days, months or years later. It also happens that we end up regretting certain decisions. Both are alright. Leadership is a continuous, mutual learning process together with those who are being led. This is regardless of whether we are talking about a single child or a company with many employees. It has to do with becoming conscious of our values and goals and exercising our leadership in agreement with these. Problem solving is part of leadership but if it takes up too much room there is a very good reason for going back and reviving the values.

# Conclusion

We have no documentation that some values are better for a family's life and experiences than others. Happy, satisfied, affectionate and dynamic families can be found everywhere in the world with a number of different values as their foundation and guiding principles. I myself could never live and thrive in many of them, but I am glad they exist. Their existence reminds me that the framework for what is considered right and wrong in this world is very wide.

There is no doubt about the fact that it is very important for parents to have some values—something they believe in, will support and that these mean something to them. Were I to sort them carefully, my criteria would be that the values must never be more important than the person. We must refrain from violating or ostracizing the individual person on the grounds of the family's values. Otherwise, they will only have value for the part of the family which has the power to violate and ostracize. This has nothing to do with family values.

The family thrives best as a place of mutual learning—not lecturing.

Lightning Source UK Ltd.
Milton Keynes UK
UKOW050405250812

198047UK00002B/17/P

9 781468 579277